Prioritize Us

Unlock Lasting Love with
One Simple, Proven Test

Nick Brancato
@PersonalDevCoach

To my Better Half—
thank you for always prioritizing us.

TABLE OF CONTENTS

Introduction 1
Aligning Love and Life Through Priorities

Chapter 1 21
What Are Life Priorities and Why They Matter?

Chapter 2 36
Taking the Prioritize Us Test—How It Works

Chapter 3 50
Self-Reflection—Understanding Your Personal Priorities

Chapter 4 70
Comparing Priorities as a Couple—The Power of Alignment

Chapter 5 92
Interpreting the Total Difference Score (TDS)

Chapter 6 117
Conflict Zones—Where Priorities Collide

Chapter 7 139
The Multi-Dimensional Nature of Priorities

Chapter 8 155
Navigating Life Changes and Evolving Priorities

Chapter 9 173
Setting Goals and Taking Action

Bonus Section 206
The Research Behind Prioritize Us

Appendix A **211**

Expanded Priority List

Appendix B **219**

Worksheets and Templates

Appendix C **226**

The Evolution of Priorities and the Timeless Role of Values

Thank You for Letting Us Be Part of Your Journey.230

About the Author **231**

Nick Brancato *231*

INTRODUCTION

Aligning Love and Life Through Priorities

Overview of the Challenge: Misaligned Priorities Create Stress, Tension, and Unmet Expectations

Most couples don't argue because they lack love—they argue because they don't agree on what matters most. It's not the disagreements themselves that cause lasting damage; it's the hidden differences in priorities lurking beneath those surface-level arguments. You might think you're arguing about household chores or finances, but those fights are often symptoms of deeper, unresolved differences about what each person believes is most important.

Take a moment to reflect: Have you ever argued with your partner about how to spend a weekend— whether to relax at home or tackle unfinished tasks? What about an argument over spending money— whether to save for the future or splurge on an experience today? On the surface, these seem like practical disagreements. But what's really going on is often much deeper:

One person is prioritizing productivity or long-term security, while the other is prioritizing relaxation or shared experiences.

Neither person is wrong—but their internal "priority maps" aren't aligned. And when those differences aren't acknowledged or discussed openly, they create frustration, tension, and unmet expectations.

The Hidden Impact of Misaligned Priorities

When couples struggle with priorities that don't align, it's not always obvious at first. The tension builds slowly—a missed conversation here, a small compromise there. Over time, those little points of friction add up, making it harder to connect emotionally.

Here's what that can look like:

- **Feeling misunderstood:** You might feel hurt when your partner doesn't seem to care about the things that matter most to you. *"I've told them how important my career is to me—why don't they support it?"*
- **Confusing arguments**: You find yourselves spiraling into conflict, even though neither of you intended to argue in the first place. *"Every time we talk about money, it feels like we're fighting—but I just want to make sure we're okay in the future."*
- **Unspoken resentment building:** When your expectations aren't met—even when they haven't been communicated clearly—resentment quietly grows. *"I shouldn't have to remind them that I want more quality time—shouldn't they know by now?"*

Over time, these unmet expectations—whether spoken or unspoken—can become emotional landmines in your relationship. Small moments of friction begin to feel like relationship roadblocks, draining your emotional energy and making even simple conversations feel exhausting.

Two Ways Misaligned Priorities Show Up in Relationships

Let's look at two common ways misaligned priorities can sneak into relationships.

1. Clashing Values in Everyday Decisions
   Imagine that Chris and Megan are trying to plan a vacation. Chris, a driven entrepreneur, is focused on career growth and thinks about the trip in terms of networking opportunities—maybe he can attend a conference along the way. Megan, on the other hand, works a high-stress job and wants to unplug and relax for the week without thinking about work at all. Neither is wrong, but they're both operating from different priorities—one is prioritizing work and ambition, and the other is prioritizing rest and connection.

This is a classic misalignment: Chris feels frustrated that Megan isn't supporting his career, and Megan feels hurt that Chris doesn't value quality time. Without open communication, this simple vacation plan can spiral into a source of conflict.

2. Long-Term Priority Drift
   Now let's take Sam and Laura, a couple married for over ten years. Early in their relationship, they were both focused on building their careers and enjoyed working long hours. But over time, Laura's priorities shifted—she

3

now values family time and wants to spend more evenings at home with their kids. Sam, however, is still in "career mode" and finds fulfillment through work, which leaves him confused and frustrated when Laura pushes for more family time.

What's happening here is something many long-term couples face: priority drift. As people grow and change, their values evolve, but they don't always communicate those changes clearly. Without regular conversations about shifting priorities, couples can slowly grow apart—not because they don't love each other, but because they're unintentionally pulling in different directions.

Why Misaligned Priorities Are So Draining

When priorities are misaligned, every decision—no matter how small—feels like a negotiation. Even small disagreements become emotional hurdles, and couples begin to feel like they're constantly pushing against each other.

The emotional impact can be significant:

- Small decisions feel overwhelming. *"Why is choosing what to eat for dinner so stressful?"*
- Long-term plans feel uncertain. *"We can't even agree on a budget—how are we supposed to plan for the future?"*
- Emotional exhaustion sets in. Partners feel disconnected, frustrated, or even defeated, wondering if they're ever going to be on the same page again.

But here's the good news: Misalignment is normal. Every couple experiences it at some point— whether they've been together for a few months or many years. The real challenge isn't having different priorities—it's learning how to identify, understand, and realign them.

A Way Forward: Tools for Realignment

The good news is that misaligned priorities don't have to lead to disconnection. With the right tools and conversations, couples can transform misalignments into opportunities for growth. This book offers a clear path forward, helping you and your partner:

- **Identify your hidden priorities:** You'll uncover what matters most to each of you—whether it's career, health, intimacy, or something else entirely.
- **Understand your differences:** You'll learn how to see your partner's priorities with curiosity, not criticism—so you can build empathy and deeper connection.
- **Create lasting alignment:** With tools found later in this book, like the Total Difference Score (TDS), you'll learn how to turn moments of friction into opportunities for deeper trust and teamwork.

Every couple will experience misalignment at some point—it's a natural part of being in a relationship.

But the difference between successful couples and those who struggle is their ability to communicate about their priorities openly and realign regularly. This book will guide you through that process, step by step.

By the end of this, you'll have the tools to stop arguing over small things, start focusing on what matters most, and build a relationship that feels intentional, fulfilling, and aligned.

Reflection Prompt

Take a moment to reflect:

- *When was the last time you felt frustrated with your partner? What unspoken priorities might have been at play beneath the surface of that moment?*
- *What do you think your partner values most right now? Are your priorities still aligned, or have they shifted in ways you haven't discussed yet?*

These are the kinds of conversations this book will help you have. The goal isn't perfect alignment— it's understanding each other better and learning how to move forward with empathy, trust, and clarity.

Why Priorities Matter: Aligned Priorities Build Emotional Connection, Trust, and Satisfaction

When couples are aligned in their priorities, something powerful happens. The relationship stops feeling like a negotiation and starts feeling like a collaborative partnership. Decisions become easier, conversations feel lighter, and the energy spent managing conflict can shift toward building connection. Instead of life being about me vs. you, it becomes about us.

But alignment isn't just about avoiding conflict—it's about creating a deeper emotional foundation for the relationship. When partners understand and support each other's priorities, trust, satisfaction, and joy flourish. The ripple effect of aligned priorities can transform every area of a relationship, from how couples communicate to how they navigate challenges together.

1. Emotional Connection: Moving From Separate Agendas to a Shared Vision

One of the most powerful outcomes of aligned priorities is the emotional connection that forms when partners are on the same page about what matters most. When you're aligned, you're no longer working from two separate agendas—you're working toward a shared vision of your life together. This sense of unity naturally deepens connection.

Even small moments of alignment—like agreeing on how to spend your weekend or planning long-term goals together—can create meaningful emotional closeness. Over time, this connection builds a sense of partnership that makes life's challenges feel more manageable.

2. Trust and Respect: Feeling Safe and Supported

- **Reduced Anxiety About Conflicts:** When you trust that your partner understands and respects your priorities, disagreements feel less threatening. You know that even if you disagree, your partner isn't dismissing what matters to you—they're just offering a different perspective. *"We may not agree on every purchase, but I trust that they respect my value of financial security."*
- **A Foundation for Resilience:** Life will inevitably throw challenges your way—whether it's a career setback, health issue, or family emergency. When couples share aligned priorities, they trust that they'll face those challenges together. *"We both know that family comes first, so I never have to wonder where we stand when things get tough."*

- **Respect for Individual Values:** Trust isn't about becoming identical or agreeing on everything. In fact, alignment means recognizing that even if you have different priorities, you still respect and support each other's values. *"My partner doesn't love working out, but they know how important it is to me—so they always encourage me to stick with it."*

3. Satisfaction and Clarity: Knowing You're Moving in the Right Direction

Couples with shared priorities report higher levels of satisfaction and fulfillment in their relationships. When both partners know what matters most—and are actively working toward those priorities—they feel a sense of clarity and purpose. Even small shifts in alignment—like compromising on how to spend time or manage money—can have a big impact on relationship satisfaction. Couples no longer feel like they're constantly negotiating, and life starts to feel more intentional and balanced.

Introducing the Prioritize Us System

This is where the Prioritize Us System comes in—a practical, easy-to-use framework that helps you and your partner uncover where your priorities align and where they diverge. It's not about scoring or judging—it's about starting meaningful conversations that bring you closer together.

At the heart of this system is the Total Difference Score (TDS), a simple tool that measures alignment between your rankings of life priorities. The TDS provides a clear snapshot of how closely your values align—and where opportunities for realignment and growth exist.

How the TDS Works: A Step-by-Step Breakdown

Using the Prioritize Us System is straightforward and accessible for any couple. You don't need any special knowledge—just an open mind and a willingness to reflect.

1. Rank Your Priorities Individually:

- Both you and your partner will receive a list of 10 core life priorities—such as Career, Finances, Relationships, Communication, and Health. Your task is to rank these priorities from 1 to 10, with 1 being the most important and 10 being the least important to you personally.
- This step is a chance to get honest with yourself. It's not about ranking what you think your partner wants to hear—it's about reflecting on what truly matters to you right now.

2. Compare Your Rankings:

- Once both partners have completed their rankings, you calculate the Total Difference Score (TDS) by measuring the difference between your rankings and your partner's rankings for each priority. For example:
  - If you rank Career as a 2 and your partner ranks it as an 8, the difference is 6 points.
  - If you both rank Health as a 1, there's no difference—0 points.
- The TDS is the sum of all these differences. The lower your TDS, the more aligned your priorities are. A higher TDS indicates more areas where you and your partner see things differently.

3. Interpreting the TDS:

- A low TDS score (below 10) signals that you and your partner are highly aligned and probably share similar values.
- A moderate TDS score (11-20) suggests that you have some alignment, but also areas that might cause friction. These areas are opportunities to better understand each other's priorities.
- A higher TDS score (above 20) indicates bigger gaps between your priorities, but that doesn't mean your relationship is doomed. Instead, it means that you have clear areas for growth, and the conversations you'll have using this system will help bridge those gaps.

A TDS of 0: A Beautifully Rare Occurrence

It's important to understand that perfection isn't the goal—and no couple is perfectly aligned all the time. In fact, the odds of having a TDS of 0 (meaning your priorities are identical) are about 1 in 13 trillion.

But here's the thing: You don't need perfect alignment to build a strong, connected relationship. A great relationship isn't about matching your partner's priorities exactly—it's about understanding the differences, respecting them, and working together intentionally. Your TDS score isn't a final verdict on your relationship—it's a starting point for deeper conversations that will bring you closer together over time.

The TDS as a Tool for Ongoing Growth

One of the biggest misconceptions about relationship tools is that you only use them once and then you're done. The Prioritize Us

System is designed to be used multiple times—it's a living framework that evolves along with your relationship.

- **Priorities Change Over Time:** As your life changes— through career shifts, parenthood, health challenges, or personal growth— your priorities will shift, too. What mattered most to you five years ago might not be as important today. That's okay. The key is to revisit your priorities regularly and adjust as needed to stay aligned. *"We used to prioritize work, travel and career advancement, but now that we have kids, family time has become a top priority."*
- **The TDS is a Conversation Starter:** The TDS isn't just a number—it's a tool that sparks meaningful conversations. When you compare your priorities, you'll have the opportunity to ask curious, open-ended questions like:
  - *"Why is health your top priority right now? I didn't realize it mattered that much to you."*
  - *"It surprised me that finances are low on your list—can you tell me more about how you're thinking about money?*

These conversations help you and your partner understand each other on a deeper level, and they create space for empathy and connection. Instead of assuming your partner doesn't care, you'll learn what drives their decisions and how to support their values.

- **Tracking Your Progress Over Time:**
  The beauty of the Prioritize Us System is that it gives you a clear way to track your progress as a couple. If your TDS score is high now, that's okay—it's just a snapshot of where you are today. As you have conversations, make adjustments, and work together toward alignment, you'll

likely see your score improve over time. And even if the number doesn't change dramatically, the way you feel about your relationship will.

The Benefits of Using the TDS System Regularly

Couples who use the Prioritize Us System aren't just checking a box—they're actively investing in their relationship. Here's how regular use of the TDS can improve your connection:

1. **Improved Communication:** When you take time to discuss your priorities, you'll naturally become better communicators—you'll learn how to listen without judgment and express your needs clearly.
2. **Deeper Trust:** As you align your priorities over time, you'll build trust—because both partners will feel seen, heard, and supported in what matters most to them.
3. **Fewer Arguments, More Clarity:** Many arguments stem from unspoken or misunderstood priorities. The TDS system brings those hidden priorities to the surface, reducing miscommunication and making decisions easier.
4. **Greater Relationship Satisfaction:** When both partners are working toward the same things—while still honoring individual priorities—the relationship feels more intentional and fulfilling.

This Isn't Just One Test—It's a Tool for Lifelong Alignment

Think of the TDS as the first step on an ongoing journey. This system isn't a one-time exercise—it's a tool you'll return to again and again throughout your relationship. Whether you're newly dating, preparing for marriage, or celebrating decades together, your priorities will evolve, and the Prioritize Us System will grow with you.

You can take the test:

- After major life changes (like a career shift, the birth of a child, or a move).
- During difficult times to uncover the root of tension.
- Annually or semi-annually as a check-in to see how your priorities are shifting over time.

Each time you revisit the TDS, you'll gain new insights and deepen your connection. The conversations you'll have along the way will help you stay aligned as a couple, no matter what life throws your way.

Reflection Prompt

- *What do you think your top 3 priorities are right now? What about your partner's? Are you confident in your guesses, or do you think you might be surprised by their answers?*

What You'll Achieve Through This Book

This book is more than just a test—it's a comprehensive roadmap for building a relationship that reflects what matters most to both of you. As you move through the chapters, you'll discover new ways to connect, grow, and create alignment, not only for the relationship you have today but for the future you want to build together. By the end of this book, you'll feel more intentional, more connected, and more confident in your ability to make decisions as a team.

1. Clarity on Your Priorities: Discover What Truly Matters

The first step toward alignment is knowing what matters most to you—and to your partner. This book will guide you through a process of self-reflection and discovery, helping you uncover your personal values and life goals. You'll no longer need to guess or assume what your partner cares about most— you'll have clarity on each other's top priorities, so you can start making choices that reflect both individual and shared values.

- **Self-Discovery:** You'll learn how to identify your personal priorities and understand how they've shaped your behavior and decisions. *"I didn't realize how much I've been prioritizing work over connection, even though I crave more quality time with my partner."*
- **Couple Alignment:** You'll also discover how your partner's priorities complement or differ from your own. Knowing where you align will make daily decisions easier—and knowing where you differ will help you navigate those differences with empathy instead of conflict.
- **The Power of Clarity:** When you both know what matters most, life becomes less about reacting to problems and more about proactively building the life you want.

Clarity is the foundation for everything else in this book—and by the time you finish, you'll have a clear picture of what you each value most.

2. Tools for Better Communication: Turn Conflict Into Connection

Every couple faces difficult conversations—about money, intimacy, family, and more. But with the right tools, these conversations don't have to be sources of stress. They can become opportunities for growth.

This book will teach you how to approach sensitive topics with curiosity, empathy, and respect. You'll learn how to listen actively without interrupting, express your needs clearly, and respond with compassion—even when the conversation feels tough. These skills will transform the way you communicate, making difficult conversations feel less like battles and more like shared problem solving.

- **Turn Arguments Into Understanding:**
  You'll learn how to identify the real issue beneath the surface—because most arguments aren't really about what you think they are. (*"We weren't fighting about chores—we were clashing over our different ideas about what 'quality time' looks like."*)
- **Build Curiosity, Not Criticism:**
  Instead of criticizing your partner's priorities, you'll discover how to ask open-ended questions that create space for deeper understanding: *"What makes that so important to you? How can I support you better in that area?"*
- **Navigate Tricky Conversations with Confidence:**
  Whether it's discussing finances, setting boundaries with family, or expressing your needs around intimacy, this book will provide conversation prompts and scripts to help you stay connected—even when the topic feels vulnerable.

By the end of this book, you'll have the communication tools you need to face any challenge as a team, building trust and connection along the way.

3. Strategies for Lasting Alignment: Stay Connected Through Life's Changes

Life doesn't stand still—and neither do your priorities. Jobs change, children grow, health challenges arise, and new opportunities come along. One of the biggest challenges couples face is staying aligned through the changing seasons of life. This book will show you how to realign your priorities regularly, so you stay connected no matter what life throws your way.

- **Adapting to Life Transitions:**
  You'll learn how to adjust your priorities as your life evolves, whether you're moving to a new city, starting a family, or navigating retirement. *"We used to prioritize adventure and travel, but now that we're parents, family time is what matters most."*
- **Regular Check-Ins for Lasting Growth:**
  This book will teach you how to revisit your priorities regularly—whether it's through annual conversations, quarterly goal-setting sessions, or monthly check-ins. These conversations will help you course-correct when necessary and ensure that you're always working toward the life you want.
- **Handling Priority Drift with Grace:**
  It's natural for partners to grow and change over time, but this book will show you how to stay connected even when your priorities shift. You'll learn how to honor each other's growth without feeling disconnected. *"Even*

*though I've shifted my focus to career growth, I
appreciate that my partner still prioritizes family time."*

The strategies in this book will ensure that your relationship stays
strong and intentional, even as your priorities evolve.

4. Practical Exercises and Actionable Steps: Make Progress Immediately

This book isn't just about ideas—it's about taking action. It
includes worksheets, conversation prompts, reflection exercises,
and tools to help you put what you've learned into practice
immediately. You won't have to wait until the end of the book to
see results—you'll start noticing positive changes from the very
first exercise.

- Worksheets for Clarity:
  Use the worksheets to rank your priorities, calculate your
  Total Difference Score (TDS), and identify areas where
  alignment is needed.
- Conversation Starters for Deeper Connection:
  Most chapters include specific conversation prompts to
  help you and your partner open up new dialogues and
  explore your priorities together.
- Goal-Setting Templates for Long-Term Success:
  You'll also find goal-setting templates and action plans to
  keep you on track as you work toward shared priorities
  and personal growth.

These tools will give you immediate wins—small but meaningful
improvements that you can feel right away. And over time, they'll
help you build the habits and systems that create lasting
alignment.

Reflection Prompt

- *What's one conversation you've been avoiding with your partner? How would it feel to approach that conversation with curiosity and empathy, knowing that your priorities are aligned?*

Let's Get Started

Whether you're just beginning your relationship or have been together for years—or even decades— Prioritize Us will help you uncover what truly matters to both of you. No matter where you are on your path, this process will give you the clarity and tools to connect on a deeper level. You don't need a perfect relationship to see results. You just need a willingness to grow together.

Why Now Is the Perfect Time

There's no perfect moment to start realigning your relationship. Life moves fast, and priorities have a way of shifting without notice. That's why now is always the right time—whether you're newly dating, engaged, married, or working through the challenges of long-term partnership.

- **If you're just starting your relationship:** Now is the time to get ahead of potential roadblocks by understanding each other's values early on. The more you align now, the easier it will be to build a foundation of trust and connection.
- **If you've been together for years:** This book will help you rediscover your priorities as a couple. As life evolves, so do your values—and this is a chance to realign and create the future you both want.

- **If you've drifted apart:** The conversations sparked by this process can bring you back to a place of connection. Realignment isn't about changing each other—it's about learning how to navigate your differences with love and empathy.

There's no need to wait for a better time. The clarity you'll gain from the Prioritize Us System can start making a difference today. Every meaningful change begins with one small step, and this test is the first step toward the relationship you both envision.

What's Possible When You Align

Imagine this:

- Making decisions together with clarity and ease, without the emotional friction of wondering if you're on the same page.
- Approaching difficult conversations—whether about money, intimacy, or family—with empathy, curiosity, and confidence.
- Feeling more connected and in sync—not because you're identical, but because you understand and respect each other's priorities.
- Celebrating the small victories of daily life—because even simple routines feel lighter when you're working from a place of alignment.

This is what's possible when you take the time to understand your priorities—and each other. Every couple experiences tension from misaligned priorities at some point—it's normal. But the difference between couples who thrive and couples who struggle is the ability to turn misalignment into an opportunity for growth.

Nick Brancato

This book will show you how to do just that. This isn't just about fixing problems or avoiding conflict— it's about creating a relationship that reflects the love and life you both want.

Reflection Prompt

Before you dive into the test, take a moment to reflect:

- *What do you hope to gain from this process?*
- *If you could align on one priority that would immediately make your relationship feel lighter, what would it be?*

This is your chance to start fresh, with clarity, purpose, and connection. Let's get started.

CHAPTER 1

What Are Life Priorities and Why They Matter?

Defining Life Priorities

Life priorities are the things we value most—those areas of life that shape our decisions, behavior, and relationships. Whether consciously or unconsciously, every action we take reflects a priority. Our priorities guide how we allocate time, energy, and resources. For example, choosing to work late rather than having dinner with your partner prioritizes career advancement or financial security over emotional connection. Similarly, spending on a vacation instead of building retirement savings shows a desire for enjoyment, adventure, or relaxation over long-term financial planning.

These priorities are neither inherently good nor bad—they are expressions of what matters most to us at a given moment. However, priorities are dynamic and can shift over time based on changing circumstances, personal growth, or external pressures. What feels critical today may become less important tomorrow. This evolving nature of priorities makes them powerful but also challenging, especially in relationships.

Nick Brancato

The complexity arises because every individual has their own unique hierarchy of priorities, shaped by personal values, experiences, and goals. Partners in a relationship may deeply love each other, but if their priorities don't align—or remain unspoken—conflict can occur. For instance, one person might prioritize financial stability through career success, while the other values emotional intimacy and quality time. Both partners might genuinely believe they are working for the good of the relationship, but because they prioritize different things, they may struggle to appreciate each other's efforts.

When priorities clash, misunderstandings, frustration, and unmet expectations often follow. One partner may feel neglected, believing their partner cares more about work, hobbies, or friends than the relationship. At the same time, the other partner may feel unappreciated, thinking their hard work goes unnoticed. These disconnects create silent tensions that slowly erode trust and emotional connection, often without either person fully recognizing the underlying cause.

However, the solution isn't to have identical priorities—it's to seek intentional alignment. Couples who understand each other's values and priorities create space for empathy, respect, and compromise. Alignment means balancing priorities in a way that reflects both partners' needs, rather than expecting one person to sacrifice their values. It's about recognizing differences as natural and learning to navigate them collaboratively.

Trust isn't just about honesty; it's also about knowing that your partner understands, supports, and respects your values. When your priorities align, you know that your partner "gets" what matters to you—even when things get difficult. This makes you feel emotionally safe within the relationship, because you trust that your partner has your back. The emotional safety that comes from aligned priorities allows couples to navigate conflict with less fear and greater empathy, creating an environment where both partners feel secure and valued.

When couples invest in aligning their priorities, they create a shared vision for the future that honors both individual and collective goals. This process fosters trust, communication, and a deeper sense of intimacy. In turn, each partner feels seen, valued, and supported—not only as part of the relationship but also as an individual.

Ultimately, understanding and aligning life priorities transforms relationships. It shifts partners from working in opposition to functioning as a team, fostering growth both within the relationship and in their personal lives.

Differences in priorities are not obstacles to love—they are opportunities to build trust and strengthen connection through mutual understanding.

The Role of Priorities in Daily Life and Long-Term Goals

Many of us move through life without consciously thinking about our priorities. We often operate on autopilot, making decisions based on habits, societal expectations, or immediate needs rather than intentionally reflecting on what truly matters.

This lack of awareness leads to unconscious priorities—the things we prioritize by default, not by choice. These unconscious priorities manifest in small, everyday ways:

- Working overtime to meet a deadline—even though you had promised to have dinner at home.
- Saying yes to social events out of obligation—when what you really need is rest and recovery.

- Avoiding difficult conversations—because discussing feelings feels uncomfortable or risky.

The challenge with these unconscious choices is that they can create internal confusion and external conflict, especially in relationships.

When neither partner is clear on what matters most—both to themselves and to each other—they may find themselves making decisions that feel misaligned with their values or the relationship's needs. Over time, this misalignment leads to frustration and tension, as partners struggle to understand why certain decisions feel disappointing or hurtful. For instance, one partner might interpret frequent overtime work as a lack of care, while the other views it as a way to provide financial security for the future.

In contrast, conscious alignment of priorities brings clarity, intention, and connection. When couples take the time to explore what each person values, they can make more intentional decisions that reflect shared goals. This could mean cutting back on work hours to prioritize family time, saving for a shared goal like a vacation or home, or intentionally scheduling alone time to recharge. These intentional choices allow partners to feel respected and understood, fostering greater trust and collaboration in both the short and long term. Life feels less chaotic, and the relationship feels like it's moving in the right direction.

This leads to the following:

- **Clear Decision-Making:** With aligned priorities, making decisions becomes easier because you know what you're working toward. "We both want to save for a house, so we're on the same page about cutting back on vacations for now."

- **A Sense of Progress:** When couples align their priorities, they feel like they're making progress together, even if challenges arise along the way. "It feels good to know that we're working toward shared goals—whether it's financial security or building a stronger family connection."
- **Greater Relationship Satisfaction:** Couples who share and respect each other's priorities experience higher levels of emotional satisfaction and long-term fulfillment. When both partners know what matters—and make intentional choices that reflect those values—they feel more confident in the direction of their relationship. "We might not have everything figured out, but knowing we're aligned on what's important gives me peace of mind."

The Power of a Shared Vision

Here's the key: When priorities are aligned, even difficult decisions become easier—because both partners are working from the same playbook. Alignment doesn't mean agreeing on every single thing; rather, it means understanding and respecting each other's values and finding ways to support both individual and shared goals.

- **Less Guesswork:** When both partners know what's important, you don't have to guess where the other person stands or worry about getting things wrong. "We both know that health is a priority, so we plan our workouts together."
- **Feeling Seen and Heard:** Alignment creates opportunities to show respect and validation for your partner's values. "They know how much family time means to me, and

they make an effort to be present with the kids every weekend."

- **Stronger Bond Through Shared Effort:** Emotional connection grows when couples work toward common goals and feel supported in their individual ones. "When my partner prioritizes my career success as much as I do, it makes me feel closer to them."

This mutual understanding allows couples to create a shared vision for the future, one that reflects the unique strengths, desires, and dreams of both partners.

A shared vision also provides clarity and stability in moments of uncertainty. When couples encounter challenges—like job changes, unexpected expenses, or personal struggles—they can rely on their aligned priorities to guide them through. Knowing what matters most helps them stay grounded and make choices that feel right, even when life gets complicated.

Ultimately, the alignment of priorities gives couples a sense of purpose and direction, transforming their relationship into a true partnership. Instead of feeling pulled in different directions or second guessing decisions, they move forward with confidence, knowing that their choices reflect the things they value most—both as individuals and as a couple.

Universal Life Priorities: The 10 Core Priorities

Every couple has a unique way of ranking and valuing life's priorities, but most people's values fall within 10 core categories. These areas reflect the fundamental aspects of life where partners either experience alignment—or encounter friction. While no two people will have the exact same priority order, understanding these categories allows couples to identify where they differ and find common ground.

Below is a deeper look at each of the 10 core priorities and the questions they raise within relationships:

1. **Career** – How much time, energy, and focus is devoted to professional goals? Career can involve everything from job satisfaction and ambition to work-life balance. Some individuals prioritize advancing their careers and see their job as a central part of their identity or purpose. Others may prefer to focus less on work and more on other areas of life, such as relationships or leisure. Couples often face tension if one person works long hours while the other values time together, especially if they struggle to communicate how work fits into their shared vision for the future.

2. **Communication** – How important is it to talk openly and consistently with your partner? Communication isn't just about the frequency of conversations; it's also about the quality and depth of those exchanges. Some individuals need regular check-ins and emotional conversations to feel connected, while others may prefer more space or communicate in different ways. Misalignment in communication styles can lead to misunderstandings, especially if one partner feels ignored or unheard.

3. **Entertainment** – How do you value leisure activities, hobbies, and downtime? How couples spend their free time can greatly affect the relationship. Some prioritize shared activities—like traveling, dining out, or watching movies—while others prefer individual hobbies. Differences in leisure preferences can create tension if one

partner feels left out or if there's an imbalance between productive time and relaxation.

4. **Finances** – What level of importance do you place on budgeting, saving, and financial security? Money is one of the most common sources of conflict in relationships. Partners may have differing views on spending vs. saving or different thresholds for financial risk. For example, one person may feel comfortable taking on debt for a vacation, while the other prefers to focus on long-term savings. Understanding each other's financial values helps couples align on budgeting, goals, and spending priorities.

5. **Growth** – How much focus do you place on personal development, learning, and self improvement? Some people are deeply committed to personal growth, whether through education, therapy, or goal-setting. Others may place more emphasis on stability and contentment in the present. Misalignment in this area can occur if one partner feels left behind by the other's growth, or if there's frustration that one person isn't as motivated to improve.

6. **Health** – How much attention do you give to physical, mental, and emotional well-being? Health priorities can range from diet and exercise routines to mental health practices like therapy or meditation. One person might prioritize fitness and healthy habits, while the other might place less importance on physical health or struggle with different health challenges. Differences in this area can affect lifestyle choices, routines, and even intimacy.

7. **Relationships** – How important are connections with family, friends, and community? The role of family, friendships, and social networks differs greatly between individuals. One partner may place a high value on

frequent family gatherings or social outings, while the other may prefer more time alone or with just their partner. Tension can arise when one partner feels overwhelmed by social obligations, or if they feel that the other isn't prioritizing relationships with loved ones.

8. **Safety** – How much emphasis do you place on security—both emotional and financial? For some, safety means emotional security—feeling supported and reassured within the relationship. For others, safety may relate more to financial stability or creating a sense of order and predictability in life. Partners may encounter challenges if one person prefers to take more risks (financial or emotional) while the other seeks a more stable, predictable environment.

9. **Sex** – What priority do you give to intimacy, physical connection, and sexual expression? Sexual intimacy plays a unique role in relationships, but partners often have different levels of desire or expectations for physical connection. While some prioritize frequent and varied sexual experiences, others may place more importance on emotional closeness than physical intimacy. Open conversations about sexual needs and expectations are key to maintaining alignment in this area.

10. **Spirituality** – How important are spiritual practices, faith, or personal meaning to you? Spirituality can take many forms, from religious practices to personal beliefs about purpose and meaning. One partner may prioritize regular church attendance or meditation, while the other may not be spiritually inclined. Misalignment here can create challenges, particularly if faith or spirituality is a core part of one partner's identity and less relevant to the other.

The Purpose of the Prioritize Us Test

These 10 priorities serve as the foundation for the Prioritize Us Test, helping couples identify and rank their personal values. The goal isn't to force partners into having identical priorities—but rather to increase awareness of what matters most to each individual. Once both partners understand each other's priorities, they can work toward intentional alignment, balancing their differences in ways that strengthen the relationship.

This alignment creates space for mutual respect and empathy, even when partners prioritize different things. By understanding where their values overlap—and where they diverge—couples can make more conscious decisions about how to spend their time, energy, and resources. Whether they are navigating daily choices or planning for long-term goals, the test encourages partners to honor both their individual and shared values.

Ultimately, the Prioritize Us Test helps couples build stronger, more intentional relationships. It offers a framework for navigating differences with clarity and cooperation—ensuring that each person feels heard, respected, and supported along the way.

Example: A Couple Discovers Their Misaligned Priorities

Let's explore how unconscious misalignment can affect even a well-intentioned couple.

Meet Sarah and Matt, a couple who have been married for five years. Their relationship is generally happy, but over time they've noticed a growing tension around how they spend their weekends. Sarah is passionate about being outdoors and views weekends as an opportunity to recharge through nature and physical activity.

Her ideal weekend includes hiking, beach trips, or long bike rides—anything that gets her moving and in the fresh air.

Matt, on the other hand, values relaxation and leisure at home. After a busy workweek, he sees weekends as the perfect time to sleep in, play video games, binge-watch movies, or unwind on the couch. Though Matt also enjoys spending time with Sarah, he prefers to recharge quietly without having to plan or engage in too many physical activities.

At first, their differences seemed harmless. Both partners loved spending time together, just in different ways. But as time went on, these differences created frustration and resentment. Sarah began to feel that Matt didn't value her love for adventure or care enough to spend meaningful time outdoors with her. Meanwhile, Matt felt pressured and exhausted by Sarah's expectations. He resented feeling like every weekend became a negotiation, and he just wanted one day to relax without any obligations.

Despite their love for each other, the couple found themselves arguing more frequently over seemingly small decisions—like whether to spend Saturday hiking or lounging at home. These disagreements left both of them feeling unheard and unappreciated, and neither could understand why the same argument kept resurfacing.

Discovering the Root of Their Misalignment Through the Prioritize Us Test

Curious to find a solution, Sarah and Matt decided to take the Prioritize Us Test, which measures how aligned (or misaligned) partners are across ten core life priorities. When they saw their Total Difference Score (TDS), the root of their conflict became clear.

The results showed that:

- Sarah ranked Health and Entertainment as her top two priorities. For her, staying active and being outdoors were essential to her physical and mental well-being. She also saw these activities as an enjoyable way to bond with Matt and create lasting memories together.
- Matt, however, ranked Entertainment much lower. For him, Communication and Finances were more important. Matt valued relaxed conversations and quiet quality time at home. His idea of connection wasn't tied to physical activity but to intimate conversations and shared downtime.

This insight helped them understand that their weekend arguments weren't really about the activities themselves—they were about their different definitions of quality time. Sarah viewed adventure as a form of meaningful connection, while Matt associated quality time with low-energy, comforting activities at home.

Finding Balance: A New Approach to Weekends

With the help of the test results, Sarah and Matt were able to shift their conversations away from blame and frustration toward collaboration and compromise. Instead of viewing their differences as a problem, they began to see them as opportunities for balance.

Using the TDS system, they created a plan that respected both of their needs:

- One weekend per month is now reserved for Sarah's outdoor adventures—whether it's a long hike or a day trip to the beach.
- One weekend per month is set aside for Matt's ideal activities—staying home, ordering takeout, and catching up on sleep or TV shows.
- On the other weekends, they work together to blend their priorities. For example, they might go for a short morning hike to honor Sarah's love for activity, followed by a movie marathon at home to give Matt the relaxed downtime he craves.

The Result: More Connection, Less Tension

The changes didn't require dramatic sacrifices—just small shifts in awareness and intentional planning. Now, instead of feeling frustrated by their differences, Sarah and Matt both feel seen, valued, and respected. Each partner knows their needs are being taken seriously, and they no longer have to compete for time or attention.

More importantly, their time together now reflects both of their priorities, which has led to a stronger emotional connection. Sarah no longer feels like Matt is dismissive of her love for the outdoors, and Matt doesn't feel pressured to meet expectations he can't sustain. By aligning their priorities, they've reduced unnecessary tension and built a more balanced, harmonious relationship.

This example highlights a powerful truth: Alignment doesn't require identical priorities—it requires mutual understanding and intentional compromise. When couples are aware of their

Nick Brancato

individual values, they can create a shared plan that honors both perspectives, making even small decisions—like how to spend a weekend—feel satisfying for both partners.

Takeaway: The Power of Awareness and Alignment

Sarah and Matt's story demonstrates how even small misalignments—like differing preferences for how to spend weekends—can slowly build tension in a relationship. What starts as minor frustrations can grow into recurring conflict if left unaddressed. But their story also highlights an important truth: awareness and intentional alignment can transform these moments of friction into opportunities for deeper connection and understanding.

The key takeaway is that you don't need identical priorities to build a meaningful and balanced relationship. In fact, expecting complete agreement on every life priority is unrealistic. What matters is understanding each other's values—and finding ways to honor and support both sets of priorities in a way that works for the relationship. The process of alignment is not about compromise in the negative sense (where one person always gives in), but about collaboration and mutual respect.

What's Next: Taking the Test and Interpreting Your Results

In the next chapter, we'll walk you step-by-step through how to take the Prioritize Us Test. We'll also guide you through how to interpret your Total Difference Score (TDS) and other insights from the test. Understanding these results will help you see exactly where alignment is strong in your relationship— and where adjustments may be needed to reduce tension and foster deeper connection.

The insights you gain will equip you to turn misalignments into opportunities for growth. Whether it's about balancing work and personal time, aligning financial goals, or creating more meaningful communication, the test gives you the tools to build a relationship rooted in mutual understanding, respect, and shared values.

CHAPTER 2

Taking the Prioritize Us Test—How It Works

The Prioritize Us Test is a simple, yet powerful tool that gives couples a clear picture of where their priorities align—and where they don't. In this chapter, we'll walk you through how to complete the test, calculate your Total Difference Score (TDS), and interpret the results so you can turn misalignment into meaningful connection.

Take the Test Individually, Then Compare Results

Each partner completes the test on their own, without discussing their answers in advance. This allows both people to reflect honestly and independently on what matters most to them, free from the influence of their partner's expectations or opinions. When both partners have completed the test, they can come together to compare their results and have meaningful discussions about where their priorities align and where they differ.

Benefits:

- Encourages private reflection and helps each person clarify their own values.
- Prevents one partner from feeling pressured to conform to the other's priorities.
- Allows for a more calm and intentional discussion when comparing results, as both partners come prepared with their insights.

Let's dive in.

Step-by-Step Walkthrough: Completing the Test and Calculating the TDS

Here's how the Prioritize Us Test works:

1. List the 10 Core Priorities:

- Career
- Communication
- Entertainment
- Finances
- Growth
- Health
- Relationships
- Safety
- Sex
- Spirituality

2. Rank the Priorities from 1 to 10:

- Each person will rank these 10 priorities from 1 (most important) to 10 (least important) based on how they feel right now.
- **For example:** If "Health" feels like the most critical part of your life, you might rank it #1. *If "Entertainment" feels less important, it might be #8 or #9.*

3. Compare Rankings Side by Side:

- Once both partners have completed their rankings, you'll compare them side by side. For each priority, calculate the difference between your rankings.

4. Calculate the Total Difference Score (TDS):

- Add up the differences for all 10 priorities to get your Total Difference Score (TDS).
- **Example:**
  - o **Health:** You rank it 2, your partner ranks it 5 Difference = 3
  - o **Finances:** You rank it 7, your partner ranks it 4 Difference = 3
  - o Total these differences across all 10 priorities to get your TDS.

5. Interpreting Your TDS Score:

- A lower TDS score means your priorities are highly aligned.
- A higher TDS score means there are more areas where your priorities differ, giving you opportunities to explore those differences together.

TDS Score Ranges and What They Mean

TDS Score	Label	What It Means
0	Symbiotic	Perfect alignment—extremely rare but possible.
1-5	Synchronized	Strong alignment with very minor differences.
6-10	Harmonized	Well-aligned with a few small differences.
11-15	Unified	Moderate alignment with room for growth.
16-20	Coordinated	Some misalignment—intentional conversations needed.
21-25	Complementary	Different priorities that need active balancing.
26-30	Divergent	Significant differences that could cause tension.
31-35	Contrasting	Major differences that may require deeper work.
36-40	Fragmented	Serious misalignment that needs immediate attention.
41-50	Polarized	Critical misalignment—

		professional guidance may help.

Alignment Isn't About Becoming Identical

It's important to remember that alignment doesn't mean agreeing on everything or becoming identical. In fact, healthy alignment leaves room for individual differences. You don't have to share every single priority—but you do need to understand and respect each other's values.

- **Example:** *"I prioritize career, while my partner values family time. But because we've talked about it openly, we've found a way to support each other's needs without feeling conflicted."*

Alignment is about intentional choices that reflect both individual and shared values. When you can have open conversations about what matters most, life becomes less about compromising reluctantly and more about co-creating a life that works for both partners.

The Ripple Effect of Alignment on Everyday Life

When couples align their priorities, the impact spreads into every aspect of their relationship. Small, everyday moments become easier and more enjoyable because both partners feel supported and understood. You'll spend less time negotiating every little thing and more time feeling connected.

- **Daily Routines Feel Smoother:** Even small decisions—like managing chores or planning your weekend—become easier because you're working from the same set of priorities. *"We both care about having a clean, peaceful space, so we divide household tasks without arguing."*

- **Long-Term Goals Feel Achievable:** With aligned priorities, big goals—like saving for a house, raising children, or planning retirement—feel less overwhelming because you're both moving in the same direction.
- **Emotional Energy Is Freed Up:** When your priorities align, you no longer feel drained by constant negotiation. Instead, your emotional energy is redirected toward connection, joy, and growth.

Even small shifts in alignment—like having regular check-ins about your priorities—can have a profound impact on your relationship. As you and your partner realign over time, life will begin to feel more harmonious and intentional.

The Beauty of Small Changes in Alignment

You don't need to be perfectly aligned to see improvements in your relationship. Even small changes in alignment can make a big difference. When couples begin to talk openly about their priorities and make intentional adjustments, they experience immediate benefits—like fewer arguments, smoother decisions, and more moments of connection.

Alignment is a dynamic process—it's not about getting everything right at once. Instead, it's about growing together, one step at a time, and building a relationship that feels intentional, balanced, and deeply connected.

41

How the Prioritize Us Test Helps Couples Align Their Priorities

The Prioritize Us Test offers a practical, structured way to identify and understand the hidden sources of tension in your relationship. Sometimes, disagreements that feel like they are about activities or decisions—like work schedules, leisure time, or finances—are really about unconscious misalignments in values. The test provides clarity by revealing where your priorities overlap and where they differ.

Once those differences are in the open, you and your partner can make intentional choices that reflect both of your values. This process isn't about changing who you are or asking your partner to abandon what matters to them—it's about working together to blend priorities in a way that strengthens your relationship.

Reflection Prompt

Think about a recent argument or disagreement you had with your partner. What priorities might have been at play beneath the surface? How would your conversation have been different if you had known each other's priorities more clearly?

Sample Rankings and Scorecards

Below is a sample of how two partners might complete the test and calculate their TDS.

Priority	Partner 1 Rank	Partner 2 Rank	Difference
Career	4	7	3
Communication	3	2	1
Entertainment	8	6	2

Finances	5	4	1
Growth	6	3	3
Health	2	2	0
Relationships	1	5	4
Safety	7	8	1
Sex	9	9	0
Spirituality	10	10	0

Total Difference Score (TDS): 3 + 1 + 2 + 1 + 3 + 0 + 4 + 1 + 0 + 0 = 15

This couple's TDS score of 15 places them in the Unified range, meaning they are moderately aligned but could benefit from intentional conversations to strengthen their connection.

What Happens After the Test?

Completing the Prioritize Us Test isn't the end of the process—it's the first step toward intentional conversations and better decision-making. The insights you gain from your TDS will act as a compass, guiding you toward areas where small adjustments can have a big impact.

With your results in hand, you'll have a clearer sense of:

- Where your priorities naturally align, creating a foundation for smooth, shared decisions.
- Where your values differ, providing opportunities to understand each other better.

- How to find balance, so that neither partner feels neglected or overburdened by competing priorities.

The test gives you the tools to move from reactive decision-making to intentional planning, helping you address tensions before they build up. Each priority you explore together will help you clarify what matters most, not just in the present but also as you plan for your future.

Turning Differences Into Opportunities for Growth

Differences in priorities don't have to create conflict—they can be valuable opportunities for growth and connection. When couples engage in open, empathetic conversations about their values, they build trust and understanding, even in the face of misalignment. The goal isn't to eliminate differences but to navigate them with respect and creativity, ensuring that both partners feel seen, heard, and supported.

Through these conversations, you'll develop a deeper understanding of your partner's needs and motivations, which will help you make more intentional decisions together. The insights from the Prioritize Us Test will guide you in building a relationship that reflects both individual and shared priorities, creating a foundation for long-term connection and fulfillment.

Using the Results to Spark Meaningful Conversations

Once you've calculated your Total Difference Score (TDS), the real benefit of the Prioritize Us Test begins: using the results to spark meaningful conversations. Your TDS isn't just a number—it's a starting point for deeper discussions about your values, expectations, and future goals. Whether your results show significant differences or strong alignment, these insights provide an opportunity to understand each other better and intentionally align your priorities.

The goal of these conversations is not to eliminate differences, but to explore them with curiosity and empathy. When partners discuss their values openly, they create space for growth, compromise, and mutual respect. Even when priorities don't perfectly align, intentional conversations can help you find creative ways to support both your individual and shared needs.

How to Approach the Conversation

- Start with curiosity, not judgment: Differences in priorities aren't inherently bad—they simply reflect unique perspectives and life experiences. Instead of trying to change your partner's priorities, approach the conversation with an open mind to better understand what drives their values.
- Focus on learning, not solving: You don't need to reach solutions immediately. Use these discussions to learn more about each other's motivations and needs without rushing to fix disagreements.
- Celebrate alignment: When you find areas where your priorities naturally align, acknowledge and appreciate those moments. These shared values are strengths that can anchor your relationship, especially during times of stress.

Conversation Starters Based on Your TDS Results

Here are some conversation prompts to help you and your partner reflect on your priorities and turn insights into meaningful dialogue:

- **"I noticed we ranked 'Career' very differently. What's driving your current focus on work?"** This prompt invites your partner to share the motivations behind their career goals. It may open up conversations about financial goals, personal fulfillment, or job-related stress. Use this as an opportunity to explore how work fits into your shared life plan and brainstorm ways to balance career demands with other priorities—like quality time or health.
- **"We both ranked 'Communication' highly—what's working well for us right now in that area?"** When you discover aligned priorities, it's important to celebrate what's going well. This prompt helps you reflect on the strengths in your communication and reinforces positive behaviors. It also gives you a chance to identify specific practices—like regular check-ins or open conversations—that are helping you stay connected, so you can continue building on that success.
- **"How do you think we could align better around 'Relationships'?"** This question encourages you to explore how each of you values relationships with family, friends, and community. It might reveal different expectations about how much time to spend with extended family, how to maintain friendships, or whether community involvement is a shared goal. The conversation can help you create a plan that honors both partners' social needs while keeping the relationship strong.

46

- "Our priorities around 'Finances' are pretty different—what would financial security look like for you?" Money is often a source of tension, and differing priorities around finances—such as saving versus spending—can lead to misunderstandings. This prompt helps you understand your partner's financial mindset and explore how you can align your financial goals (like saving for a home or taking vacations) in a way that feels good to both of you.
- "We ranked 'Health' differently. How can we better support each other's well-being?" Health priorities often reflect different lifestyles and routines. Maybe one of you prioritizes physical fitness, while the other focuses more on mental health. This conversation can help you discover ways to support each other's self-care practices, whether through shared workouts, meal planning, or encouraging rest when needed.

Creating an Action Plan for Alignment

Once you've discussed your TDS results, it's time to turn insights into action. You don't need to align perfectly on every priority, but you can create a plan that respects both partners' values.

Here are a few steps to help you move forward:

1. **Identify your shared priorities:** Start by highlighting the priorities where your values already align. These areas are strengths to build on and can serve as a foundation for future decisions.
2. **Discuss trade-offs:** For priorities that differ, talk about how you can balance them intentionally. For example, if one of you prioritizes leisure and the other values productivity, you might decide to alternate between

weekends spent relaxing and weekends focused on completing projects.

3. **Make small adjustments:** Alignment doesn't require drastic changes. Look for small ways to honor each other's priorities in daily life. For example, if health is important to one partner, you could schedule morning walks together or prepare healthy meals as a team.

4. **Revisit your priorities regularly:** Life circumstances and values shift over time, so it's important to check in periodically to make sure your priorities are still aligned. Set aside time every few months to review your priorities and make any necessary adjustments.

What Comes Next: The Power of Self-Reflection

In the next chapter, we'll take a deeper dive into the importance of self-reflection—an essential step toward achieving lasting alignment with your partner. Before you can fully align your priorities as a couple, it's important to understand your own values and how they shape your actions, expectations, and goals.

Self-reflection allows you to:

- Clarify your personal priorities, so you can express them clearly to your partner.
- Identify areas where your priorities may have shifted, especially during life transitions (like career changes or parenthood).
- Recognize habits or assumptions that might unintentionally create tension.

Through self-reflection, you'll gain insights that will make your conversations with your partner more productive and meaningful.

When both partners are aware of their own values and needs, it becomes much easier to align intentionally—not by forcing compromises but by finding solutions that honor both perspectives.

Intentional Love and Alignment Begins Here

Taking the Prioritize Us Test is the first step in a lifelong process of building intentional love and aligned priorities. Relationships are always evolving, and priorities will shift as you navigate new phases of life together. It isn't about achieving perfect alignment once and for all—it's about learning how to adjust, adapt, and communicate openly along the way.

As you move forward, remember that alignment isn't the absence of differences—it's the presence of mutual understanding. When you and your partner are committed to listening, learning, and balancing priorities, you'll build a relationship that reflects both your individual identities and your shared vision for the future.

Now, let's dive into the next chapter and discover how understanding yourself is the key to creating alignment with your partner. The path toward deeper connection, better decisions, and lasting love begins with knowing yourself—and we're here to help you every step of the way.

CHAPTER 3

Self-Reflection— Understanding Your Personal Priorities

Before you and your partner can successfully align your priorities, you must first understand your own. Building a relationship rooted in mutual respect and intentional alignment starts with each person developing self-awareness—the ability to reflect on what truly matters and how those values shape your decisions and behavior. Without this clarity, it becomes challenging to express your needs clearly or recognize how misalignments may be affecting your relationship.

This chapter focuses on the importance of getting in tune with your personal priorities. When you understand yourself, it not only strengthens your sense of identity but also lays the groundwork for healthy communication with your partner. Knowing your priorities helps you make choices that align with your values and ensures that your relationship reflects who you are as an individual, not just as a partner.

Why Self-Awareness is Essential for Alignment

Self-awareness isn't just about knowing what you like or dislike—it's about understanding the deeper values that drive your behavior and recognizing how those values show up (or fail to) in your everyday life. If you don't know what your priorities are, it's easy to act on autopilot, making decisions based on habit, cultural expectations, or the opinions of others. This can lead to frustration when your life—or relationship—feels out of sync with what you truly value.

When partners take time to reflect on their own values, it makes it easier to:

- Communicate openly about their priorities without confusion or mixed signals.
- Identify potential areas of misalignment and address them early, before they cause tension.
- Make intentional decisions about how to balance individual needs with shared goals.

Without this foundation of self-awareness, it's easy to project unmet expectations onto your partner, creating misunderstandings. For example, you might assume your partner doesn't value the relationship when, in reality, you've been neglecting your own need for quality time and haven't clearly communicated it.

Alignment starts with you—when you know what matters to you, you make it easier for your partner to understand and support your priorities.

Nick Brancato

How to Identify Your Personal Priorities

Getting clear on your priorities requires honest reflection. It's not always easy to sort out what you truly value versus what you feel you "should" value based on external pressures. Below are some steps to help you uncover your personal priorities and recognize whether your daily actions reflect those values.

1. Reflect on What Matters Most to You

Ask yourself:

- What activities, relationships, or goals make me feel most fulfilled?
- Which areas of my life feel most important right now—career, family, health, creativity, or something else?
- If I could only focus on three things for the next year, what would they be?

These questions will help you focus on the values that bring you joy, purpose, and meaning, giving you insight into what matters most to you.

2. Notice How You Spend Your Time and Energy

Your true priorities aren't just in your thoughts—they show up in how you spend your time, energy, and resources. Take a moment to reflect on how your daily actions align (or don't align) with the values you identified.

- Are you spending more time at work than with loved ones, even though relationships are a top priority?

- Are you neglecting self-care because you're focusing too much on external responsibilities?
- Do your spending habits reflect your long-term financial goals, or are you making impulsive choices?

The way you spend your time and energy reveals your actual priorities, which may or may not align with what you think your values are. This awareness helps you adjust your behavior so your actions reflect what matters most.

3. Identify Conflicting Priorities

Sometimes, life presents you with competing priorities—and that's okay. For example, you might value both career growth and family time, but they can occasionally pull you in different directions.

Reflecting on these internal conflicts can help you make intentional decisions about when to prioritize one value over another. Recognizing these tensions also helps you communicate them clearly to your partner so they can support you more effectively.

Communicating Your Priorities to Your Partner

Once you've identified your priorities, the next step is to communicate them openly with your partner. The more specific and honest you are about what matters to you, the easier it will be for your partner to understand your needs and make aligned decisions.

- **Be specific:** Instead of saying, "I value health," explain what that means to you: "I need time to work out three times a week because it helps me manage stress."

- **Share your motivations:** Let your partner know why certain things are important to you. For example, "I want to save more money because financial security helps me feel safe and reduces my anxiety."
- **Ask for support:** Alignment isn't just about stating your priorities—it's about working together. Ask your partner how they can support your goals and discuss how you can balance each other's needs.

When partners communicate their priorities clearly and without judgment, it fosters trust and empathy, creating a foundation for intentional alignment.

The Importance of Self-Awareness

Self-awareness is the foundation of intentional living and aligned relationships. It involves understanding your core values, desires, and goals—and how these elements show up (or fail to show up) in your daily life. Without this clarity, it's easy to slip into habits or routines that don't align with what truly matters to you. You may say yes to things that drain your energy or pursue goals that no longer hold meaning, leaving you feeling disconnected from yourself and dissatisfied in your relationship.

How Lack of Self-Awareness Impacts Relationships

In relationships, a lack of self-awareness often leads to miscommunication, frustration, and unmet expectations. If you're not clear on your own priorities, it's unrealistic to expect your partner to intuitively understand or support them. This can result in misunderstandings—where one person feels neglected, and the other feels unappreciated.

For example:

- You may prioritize alone time to recharge but feel guilty asking for it because you haven't communicated that need to your partner.
- Your partner may interpret your busyness as disinterest in the relationship, when in reality, you're focused on personal goals you haven't expressed clearly.

Similarly, conflict often arises when one partner is honoring their priorities, but their actions seem confusing or inconsiderate to the other person. For instance, if career growth is important to you and you've taken on extra work hours, but your partner values quality time, tension can build if those priorities aren't communicated openly. Misunderstandings like these erode trust over time, leading to unnecessary conflict.

However, the good news is that once you become aware of your own values, it becomes much easier to express them clearly and invite your partner into a conversation about how to align your priorities intentionally.

The Impact of Misalignment Within Yourself

Self-awareness isn't just about recognizing what you value—it's also about identifying when your actions don't align with your stated priorities. It's easy to say that certain things matter to you, but your behavior might tell a different story. Noticing these internal misalignments is the first step toward realignment, both in your personal life and your relationship.

For example:

- You might say that health is a priority, but if you regularly skip workouts and rely on fast food, your actions aren't supporting that value.
- You might believe that personal growth matters to you, but if you haven't pursued learning opportunities or taken time for reflection, there's a gap between your intentions and your actions.

These internal misalignments can create frustration and self-doubt, which can spill over into your relationship. If you feel disconnected from your own values, you may become more irritable, anxious, or critical—leading to tension with your partner. Recognizing these gaps helps you take small, intentional steps toward realignment, improving both your well-being and your relationship dynamics.

How Self-Awareness Strengthens Relationships

When you know yourself well, you bring clarity, honesty, and intention into your relationship. This self-awareness allows you to:

- Communicate your needs and priorities clearly, without relying on your partner to guess or assume what matters to you.
- Recognize your partner's efforts more easily because you know what support looks like for you— and can ask for it directly.
- Navigate conflicts from a place of understanding, rather than frustration or resentment, because you're aware of the priorities driving your behavior.

For example, instead of saying, "You never spend time with me," you might say, "Quality time is really important to me, and I feel disconnected when we don't have enough of it." This shift in language makes your priorities clear to your partner and helps build empathy and trust.

The Power of Trust and Openness Through Self-Awareness

Self-awareness doesn't just improve communication—it also lays the groundwork for trust and openness in your relationship. When you understand your values and align your actions accordingly, your partner sees that you are living with integrity. This creates a sense of emotional safety—your partner can trust that you will express your needs honestly and listen to theirs with the same openness.

Additionally, when both partners bring self-awareness into the relationship, it becomes easier to embrace differences without feeling threatened. You can recognize that differences in priorities aren't personal attacks—they're just reflections of unique values and needs. With this perspective, you and your partner can co-create solutions that honor both sets of priorities, leading to intentional alignment.

Self-Awareness as a Foundation for Alignment

Ultimately, self-awareness is the key to creating alignment—both within yourself and with your partner. When you know what you value and take intentional steps to align your behavior with those values, you show up more authentically in your relationship. This authenticity makes it easier to communicate, compromise, and collaborate with your partner.

By bringing clarity and intention into your relationship, you create a space where both partners feel seen, heard, and respected. Rather than reacting emotionally to differences or unmet expectations, you can respond thoughtfully, guided by a deep understanding of your own values. This makes alignment a shared journey—not a demand for conformity, but a process of balancing individual needs with shared goals.

Self-awareness empowers you to:

- Live more intentionally, reducing stress and frustration.
- Communicate effectively, improving connection with your partner.
- Build trust and empathy, creating a foundation for long-term alignment.

When both partners bring clarity, honesty, and intention into the relationship, alignment becomes not just possible—but sustainable.

Personal Reflection Exercise: Identifying Strengths and Misalignments

This exercise will help you gain clarity about your current priorities and notice where your actions align or conflict with your values. It's a simple but powerful way to assess whether the life you are living reflects what matters most to you. Misalignments are a natural part of life—identifying them isn't about perfection but about creating awareness and intention moving forward.

Take some time to sit with these questions, reflecting honestly. Use a journal or notebook to write down your thoughts. This process works best when you're open and nonjudgmental with yourself. If you uncover areas that feel off-balance or neglected, that's okay—awareness is the first step toward realignment.

Guided Questions for Self-Reflection

1. **What are your top 3 priorities right now?** (*Think about the areas of life that feel most important to you—Career, Health, Relationships, etc.*)

- Which priorities are at the forefront of your mind?
- Have these shifted recently due to life changes (e.g., starting a new job, becoming a parent, or facing health challenges)?
- Are these priorities based on your genuine values, or are they influenced by external pressures (like family expectations or social norms)?

Why this matters: Identifying your top priorities helps you focus on what matters most in your life right now. Life circumstances change, so your priorities will evolve too. This question allows you to reconnect with your current values and see if your actions reflect them.

2. **Where do you feel most satisfied in life?** (*Which areas bring you joy, fulfillment, or peace?*)

- What parts of your life feel aligned with your values?
- Which relationships, activities, or habits make you feel most grounded or fulfilled?
- When do you experience a sense of peace or flow, where things feel effortless and meaningful?

Why this matters: Recognizing your areas of satisfaction helps you celebrate what's working well. These are the strengths you can build on to bring more balance into other areas. It also reinforces the value of gratitude—taking time to acknowledge what's going right encourages further growth.

3. **Which areas of your life feel out of balance or neglected?** *(Are there priorities you've pushed to the side or haven't had time to focus on?)*

- Are there aspects of your life that feel overwhelming or out of control?
- Is there something you care about that you've deprioritized recently—like a hobby, relationship, or self-care routine?
- What have you been meaning to focus on, but haven't found the time or energy to prioritize?

Why this matters: Identifying areas that feel neglected helps you pinpoint where realignment is needed. Sometimes, small shifts—like setting boundaries at work or scheduling time for yourself—can bring greater balance and fulfillment.

4. **Do your daily actions reflect your top priorities?** *(For example: If "Health" is a top priority, are you making time for exercise and self-care?)*

- How are your daily routines and habits supporting (or not supporting) your priorities?
- Are there gaps between what you say you value and how you spend your time?
- Are there recurring patterns or distractions (like social media or work stress) that pull you away from your values?

Why this matters: This question encourages you to align your behavior with your values. It's common to get caught up in routines that don't reflect your priorities—becoming aware of these gaps helps you take intentional action to realign your day-to-day life.

5. **What habits or routines are out of sync with your values?**
   (Are there things you're doing out of obligation or habit that no longer serve you?)

   - Are you saying yes to activities or obligations that drain your energy?
   - Are there habits or commitments you've held onto because of guilt, fear, or social pressure, even though they no longer feel meaningful?
   - Do you feel stuck in routines that feel automatic rather than intentional?

Why this matters: This question helps you recognize which habits are keeping you stuck and which ones are worth letting go of. Releasing habits that no longer serve you creates space for new ones that better reflect your priorities and values.

6. **What is one area of your life where you'd like to make a change?** *(Where could you shift your time, energy, or focus to better align with your values?)*

   - Which area feels most urgent or meaningful to address?
   - If you made one small change—like setting a boundary, practicing self-care, or investing in a relationship—how would it impact your well-being?
   - What first step could you take today to move toward that change?

Why this matters: Change doesn't have to be overwhelming. This question helps you focus on one actionable shift that would have the greatest impact on your well-being. Small, intentional changes can create momentum toward realignment, bringing your actions back in line with your values.

Reflection Without Judgment

As you work through these questions, be kind to yourself. It's common to find areas of misalignment, and this isn't a sign of failure—it's a normal part of life. Priorities shift, life gets busy, and it's easy to lose sight of what matters most. The purpose of this reflection exercise isn't to achieve perfection but to cultivate awareness and empower yourself to take intentional action.

Aligning Actions with Values: Realigning Your Life

Once you've identified your priorities, the next step is to align your actions with those values. When your daily behaviors reflect what truly matters to you, life feels more meaningful and intentional. You experience less stress, more fulfillment, and a deeper connection to yourself and the people around you. However, alignment isn't about striving for perfection—it's about making deliberate choices that honor your values, even in small ways.

Life can pull us in many directions, making it easy to drift into habits or routines that don't reflect our priorities. Realigning your actions with your values helps you live more authentically and intentionally, ensuring that your time, energy, and focus go toward what matters most. Below are practical steps to help you bring your actions into alignment with your values.

1. Identify One Small Change at a Time

It's tempting to want to overhaul your entire life when you notice areas of misalignment, but trying to change too much at once can lead to burnout. Start small by focusing on one specific area where your actions don't align with your values.

- **Example:** If health is a top priority, but you haven't been exercising, commit to adding a 10-minute morning walk a few times a week. Or, if you've been eating out too often, meal-prep on Sundays to make healthier food choices easier.
- **Why it works:** Small, consistent actions build momentum over time. Even minor changes can create a ripple effect, leading to larger shifts in alignment.

Tip: Choose a change that feels doable—something small enough that you can start immediately but meaningful enough to move the needle toward alignment.

2. Say No to Things That Don't Align

Saying yes to every request, project, or obligation often means saying no to yourself. Realigning your actions with your values requires learning how to set boundaries and let go of commitments that don't support your priorities. This can feel uncomfortable, especially if you're used to people-pleasing or saying yes out of obligation.

- **Ask yourself:** When an opportunity or request arises, take a moment to reflect: "Does this align with my priorities?" If the answer is no, consider whether you can politely decline or delegate the task.
- **Example:** If family time is a priority, but a colleague asks you to work late, it's okay to say no and protect your evening for your family.

Tip: Practice saying no with kindness and confidence: "Thank you for thinking of me, but I can't commit to this right now." Over time, this will help you feel more empowered to make choices that align with your values.

3. Create Habits That Support Your Values

The key to sustainable alignment is embedding your values into your daily routines. When you create habits that reflect your priorities, you make it easier to stay connected to what matters—without relying on motivation or willpower.

- **Example:** If relationships are important to you, schedule a weekly date night with your partner or set a reminder to call a friend or family member every week.
- If personal growth is a priority, carve out 15 minutes a day for reading, journaling, or meditation.

By turning your priorities into habits, they become a natural part of your life rather than something you have to think about constantly. Small, intentional routines help you stay on track—even when life gets busy.

Tip: Start with one habit at a time and anchor it to something you already do. For example, if you want to meditate daily, pair it with your morning coffee or before bed.

4. Track Your Progress and Celebrate Small Wins

Realigning your life with your values isn't a one-and-done task—it's an ongoing process that requires consistent reflection and adjustment. Take time to check in with yourself regularly to see how well your actions align with your priorities.

- **Example:** Set aside time weekly or monthly to review your habits, decisions, and commitments. Ask yourself:
    - Are my actions still aligned with my values?
    - Have my priorities shifted, and if so, do I need to adjust my routines?

Celebrating small wins is also important. Realignment can feel like a slow process, but each step you take toward living intentionally deserves recognition. Whether it's sticking to your new habit for a week or saying no to something that doesn't align, acknowledge your progress and reward yourself.

Tip: Keep a progress journal or checklist to track the small changes you've made. When you see how far you've come, it reinforces your commitment to intentional living.

Realignment: A Lifelong Practice

Realigning your actions with your values is a lifelong journey, not a destination. As your circumstances, goals, and relationships evolve, your priorities will also shift. The key is to remain flexible and self-aware—checking in with yourself regularly to ensure your actions continue to reflect what matters most.

Remember, perfection isn't the goal—progress is. Even when life gets busy or messy, the small, intentional steps you take will add up over time, helping you create a life that feels more meaningful and aligned.

By making deliberate choices, setting boundaries, and building supportive habits, you'll stay connected to your priorities—and, in turn, reduce stress, increase fulfillment, and deepen your connection to both yourself and others.

Worksheet: Identifying Time and Energy Misalignments

This worksheet is designed to help you gain clarity on how you're currently spending your time and energy and assess whether those efforts align with your stated priorities. It's easy to get caught up in routines and commitments that don't reflect what truly matters to you. By examining where your resources are going, this exercise will provide insight into areas of misalignment and help you identify practical steps for realignment.

Use the following steps to track your time and energy, evaluate your priorities, and make intentional adjustments.

Step 1: Fill in the Table Below

Think about how you typically spend your time and energy during an average week. In the table below, list the estimated hours spent on each category and assign a priority ranking from 1 to 10, with 1 being "most important" and 10 being "least important." Be honest with yourself—this exercise works best when you reflect accurately on your current habits.

Category	Hours Spent Weekly	How Important Is This to Me? (Rank 1-10)
Career		
Communication (e.g., conversations, social check-ins)		
Entertainment (e.g., TV, games, social outings)		
Finances (e.g., budgeting, managing money)		
Growth (e.g., learning, personal development)		

Health (e.g., exercise, sleep, nutrition)		
Relationships (e.g., time with family, friends, or partner)		
Safety (e.g., emotional or financial security efforts)		
Sex (e.g., intimacy, physical connection)		
Spirituality (e.g., prayer, meditation, religious activities)		

Step 2: Evaluate Your Results

Now that you've filled in the table, reflect on any gaps between how you're currently spending your time and how important each area is to you. Use the questions below to help guide your reflection:

- Are there areas where you're spending too much time and energy on things that don't feel important to you?
    - **Example:** You're spending several hours a week on social media or entertainment, but these activities rank low in importance.
    - **Insight:** This may be a sign that certain habits or distractions are pulling you away from more meaningful pursuits.

- Are there areas you're neglecting, even though they rank high in importance?
  - **Example:** You identified health or relationships as a top priority, but you're only spending minimal time on exercise or quality time with loved ones.
  - **Insight:** This suggests that rebalancing your schedule could improve your overall satisfaction and well-being.

Tip: Look for patterns. Are there low-priority areas consuming most of your time? Are high-priority areas getting crowded out by work, entertainment, or obligations? Recognizing these patterns will help you identify where your time and energy adjustments are needed.

Step 3: Take One Action Toward Realignment

Choose one small, practical action you can take this week to better align your time and energy with your stated priorities. It's important to start small—even a minor shift can make a big difference. Write down your action below to help keep yourself accountable.

Example: "I will block out one hour on Sunday to meal prep, so I have healthy lunches ready for the week."

Alignment is a Process, Not a One-Time Fix

This worksheet isn't about immediate perfection—it's about bringing awareness to how you spend your time and making intentional adjustments. Realignment is an ongoing process that requires regular reflection and adjustment. As your circumstances shift, you may need to reevaluate your priorities and tweak your routines.

Consider repeating this exercise every few months to stay on track. Each time you do, you'll gain new insights and discover small improvements that help you live a more aligned and meaningful life.

Remember, the goal isn't to do everything perfectly—it's to move toward alignment one intentional step at a time. Every small adjustment you make brings you closer to living a life that reflects your true values and helps you feel more fulfilled, connected, and at peace.

What's Next: Comparing Your Priorities as a Couple

Understanding yourself is just the first step—now it's time to bring that understanding into your relationship. In the next chapter, we'll explore how to compare your priorities as a couple and use the Total Difference Score (TDS) system to identify areas of alignment and misalignment.

This process isn't about forcing identical priorities—it's about understanding each other's values and finding ways to balance both partners' needs intentionally. You'll learn how to use the TDS as a tool for growth, uncovering hidden sources of tension and discovering new ways to align your priorities in ways that work for both of you.

When couples work toward alignment with openness and intention, the result is a relationship where both people feel valued and supported—a partnership built on mutual understanding, shared goals, and trust.

Let's move forward toward intentional love—building a life together that reflects both who you are as individuals and what you want to create as a couple.

CHAPTER 4

Comparing Priorities as a Couple—The Power of Alignment

Understanding your own priorities is the first step—but the real magic happens when you compare your priorities with your partner's and start working toward alignment. This process reveals where you and your partner are already in sync and where your differences lie. These insights provide opportunities to deepen connection, reduce tension, and make intentional decisions that reflect both your values.

How Misaligned Priorities Impact Relationships

Even in strong, loving relationships, differences in values can lead to conflict if they aren't acknowledged and managed intentionally. These differences don't mean the relationship is broken— misalignment is natural. However, when partners aren't aware of each other's priorities, or when those priorities clash, unspoken frustrations and unmet needs can build over time. Many recurring arguments in relationships aren't really about surface-level issues—they reflect deeper misalignments in values and priorities.

Learning to recognize and respect these differences is essential. By doing so, couples can avoid misunderstandings and resentment, allowing them to work together toward intentional alignment. Below are some common challenges that arise from misaligned priorities, along with insights into how these conflicts unfold.

1. Time Management Conflicts

The Issue: One partner may prioritize career growth and feel that working overtime or taking on extra responsibilities is necessary for personal success or financial security. Meanwhile, the other partner may value quality time and feel frustrated by the lack of attention or connection in the relationship.

How It Plays Out:

- The partner focused on career advancement may believe they are working for the benefit of the relationship (e.g., earning more income or building a secure future).
- Meanwhile, the partner who values time together might feel neglected or unimportant, leading to arguments about priorities and unmet emotional needs.

Result:

- Frequent arguments about spending too much time at work or not prioritizing the relationship.
- Both partners feel misunderstood—one feels pressured to scale back at work, while the other feels emotionally abandoned.

Insight: The conflict isn't really about the time spent working—it's about how both partners assign different meanings to time.

2. Financial Disagreements

The Issue: Money can be a major source of tension in relationships, especially when partners prioritize spending and saving differently. One partner may value financial security and prefer to save for the future, while the other believes in spending money on experiences, such as travel, hobbies, or dining out, to make life enjoyable now.

How It Plays Out:

- The partner focused on saving might view the other as reckless or irresponsible with money.
- The partner who prioritizes experiences may feel restricted or controlled by a focus on savings, leading to frustration.
- Both partners might believe their approach is in the best interest of the relationship, making it harder to see the other's perspective.

Result:

- Arguments over budgeting and how money should be spent.
- Both partners feel misunderstood—one may feel financially insecure, while the other feels deprived of meaningful experiences.

Insight: The tension isn't really about the money—it's about different beliefs about what creates happiness and security.

3. Intimacy and Emotional Connection

The Issue: In some relationships, partners place different levels of importance on physical intimacy and emotional connection. One partner might prioritize sex and physical touch as a key way to feel loved and connected, while the other may place more value on communication, trust, and emotional closeness.

How It Plays Out:

- The partner who values physical intimacy may feel rejected or unwanted if sex isn't prioritized.
- The other partner may feel that emotional closeness— through conversations or shared activities— is more meaningful and necessary before physical intimacy can happen.
- Over time, both partners may feel unfulfilled—one craving more intimacy, the other craving more emotional connection.

Result:

- Resentment and frustration build, with both partners feeling that their needs aren't being met.
- Misalignment in these areas can cause distance and lead to misunderstandings about what love and connection mean to each partner.

Insight: The conflict isn't about sex versus communication—it's about how each person expresses and experiences love differently.

4. Growth vs. Stability Conflicts

The Issue: Some couples struggle when one partner prioritizes personal growth (such as learning, self-improvement, or pursuing new goals) while the other prefers stability, comfort, and routine.

How It Plays Out:

- The partner focused on growth may feel held back by their partner's preference for consistency.
- Meanwhile, the partner who values stability might feel stressed or overwhelmed by constant change, seeing it as a disruption to the relationship's balance.
- This dynamic can create a push-pull tension, with one partner wanting to pursue new experiences and the other wanting to maintain the status quo.

Result:

- Frustration builds over time, as the growth-oriented partner feels stifled, and the stability-oriented partner feels unsettled.
- Both partners may feel unappreciated for their efforts— one for wanting to grow, the other for maintaining consistency and security.

Insight: The conflict isn't about change versus routine—it's about different perspectives on what brings fulfillment and peace.

The Path to Alignment: Recognizing and Respecting Differences

The goal in relationships isn't to eliminate differences in priorities—every couple will have them. In fact, these differences can enrich your relationship by offering diverse perspectives and strengths. However, unacknowledged or unmanaged misalignments can lead to conflict, resentment, and unmet needs over time. The key is to recognize and respect these differences, communicate openly about them, and find ways to balance your priorities intentionally.

Strategies for Managing Misaligned Priorities

1. **Communicate Regularly:** Open conversations about priorities help each partner understand what matters most to the other. This prevents misunderstandings and allows both partners to feel seen and valued.
2. **Compromise Without Sacrifice:** Intentional alignment doesn't mean one partner has to abandon their priorities. Instead, it involves finding creative solutions where both people's needs are honored.
3. **Revisit Priorities Periodically:** Life circumstances change, and so do priorities. Make it a habit to check in regularly to ensure that both partners' priorities are still aligned— or adjust when necessary.
4. **Find Shared Values:** Look for overlapping priorities that both partners can focus on together. For example, if one partner values stability and the other values personal growth, you might work together to create a structured plan for growth that feels stable and manageable.
5. **Appreciate the Differences:** Instead of seeing differences as obstacles, view them as opportunities to grow together. Each partner brings unique values and strengths to the relationship, which can lead to a more balanced, dynamic partnership.

Taking the Test: Identifying Alignment and Misalignment

Taking the Prioritize Us Test is a powerful way to bring clarity and foster deeper understanding in your relationship. Often, misunderstandings arise because partners assume they share the same priorities—only to discover that they view certain aspects of life very differently. This process allows both of you to compare your values side by side and opens the door to insightful conversations about how your priorities shape your actions and decisions.

Rather than focusing on who is "right" or "wrong," the goal of this exercise is to recognize areas of alignment and misalignment and use those insights to strengthen your connection. By approaching differences with curiosity and openness, you'll gain a clearer picture of each other's needs, fostering mutual respect and intentional alignment moving forward.

Step 1: Rank the Priorities Separately

The first step is for each partner to complete the 10-priority ranking independently. This ensures that both of you take time to reflect honestly on what matters most in your life, without being influenced by your partner's responses.

- **Why it matters:**
  Taking time for individual reflection encourages you to connect with your personal values and recognize any shifts in your priorities. Life circumstances—such as career changes, health challenges, or new family roles— can influence what feels most important at any given time. Independent reflection ensures that you can express yourself authentically in the process.

Step 2: Compare Results Side by Side

After both partners have completed their rankings, it's time to compare your results side by side. Lay out your answers together and calculate your Total Difference Score (TDS).

- For each priority, note the differences between your rankings. The greater the difference, the more it indicates an area worth discussing. This doesn't mean you need to eliminate the difference —it simply suggests that this priority might require more intentional alignment in your relationship.
- **TDS Tip:** A high TDS score doesn't mean your relationship is in trouble—it simply highlights opportunities for growth. Likewise, a low TDS score doesn't mean you won't encounter disagreements. The goal is to build understanding around each other's priorities and find ways to balance both individual and shared values.

Step 3: Identify Key Areas of Alignment

Start the conversation on a positive note by focusing on the priorities where your rankings are similar. These shared values are strengths in your relationship—points of alignment that likely make decisions in these areas smoother and less stressful.

- Celebrate your alignment:
  Recognizing where your values align builds trust and connection, reinforcing the idea that you are a team working toward shared goals. For example:
  - "We both ranked Health as a top priority. No wonder we've been feeling good about our new exercise routine!"

o "We both value Communication highly. That's probably why we've been able to resolve conflicts more easily lately."

Starting with alignment sets a positive tone and helps create a sense of collaboration, which makes it easier to navigate areas of misalignment when the time comes.

Step 4: Discuss Misaligned Priorities with Curiosity

Now, shift your focus to the priorities where your rankings differ the most. This is where the real work— and the real growth— begins. Differences in priorities aren't necessarily bad; they simply reflect the fact that you're two unique individuals with different experiences, needs, and perspectives. The key is to approach these conversations with curiosity rather than judgment.

- **Ask open-ended questions:** Instead of assuming why your partner ranked a priority higher or lower, invite them to share their thoughts. This helps both of you understand the deeper meaning behind each priority.
- **Example Questions:**
  - "I noticed you ranked Career a lot higher than I did—can you tell me more about what that means to you?"
    - This invites your partner to explain their current focus on work. They might share that they're working toward a promotion or that they feel career success provides a sense of security for the future.

- o "I ranked Relationships higher than you did—do you think we're spending enough quality time with family and friends?"
  - This opens a dialogue about what quality time means to each of you. One partner may prefer fewer social events, while the other thrives on community connection.

Navigating Differences with Empathy and Respect

When discussing misalignments, it's important to acknowledge each other's perspectives without trying to "fix" them. Your partner's priorities may reflect different needs or life experiences that you haven't fully understood yet. By listening actively, you'll gain a deeper appreciation for their values and motivations.

- **Tip:** Try using phrases like "I hadn't thought of it that way" or "That makes a lot of sense now that you explain it" to show your partner that you're listening and respecting their point of view.
- **Focus on balancing priorities, not changing them:** The goal isn't to force your partner to change their priorities to match yours—it's about finding creative ways to support both partners' values. For example:
  - o If one partner prioritizes Career while the other prioritizes Relationships, you might agree to designate specific times for uninterrupted connection, even during a busy workweek.

What If Your Priorities Don't Align Perfectly?

It's common for couples to have some differences in their priorities, and that's okay. Perfect alignment isn't necessary for a successful relationship. The key is to understand each other's values and intentionally find a balance that works for both of you. This could mean:

- **Taking turns prioritizing different needs:** For example, one weekend could be devoted to relaxing at home (reflecting one partner's preference for downtime) and the next weekend could be spent outdoors (reflecting the other partner's love of adventure).
- Creating shared rituals that honor both partners' values, such as meal prepping together to support health while also using that time to connect and communicate.

Using the Test as a Tool for Growth

Taking the Prioritize Us Test isn't just about identifying alignment and misalignment—it's about using those insights to grow closer as a couple. The conversations sparked by the test help you:

- Appreciate your differences and see them as opportunities to grow together.
- Build empathy and trust by learning more about your partner's values.
- Develop intentional strategies to balance individual and shared priorities.

Actionable Advice: Steps to Begin Constructive Conversations

Once you've compared your results and identified areas of alignment and misalignment using the Prioritize Us Test, the next step is to discuss what your TDS score reveals. These conversations can help you and your partner deepen your understanding of each other's values and create intentional plans for aligning your priorities. The key to success is approaching these discussions with curiosity, empathy, and collaboration—rather than judgment or frustration.

Below are six practical steps to help guide these important conversations.

1. Start with a Positive Mindset

Before diving into areas of misalignment, begin by acknowledging the priorities where your values align. Celebrating these shared strengths reinforces the positive foundation of your relationship and sets a cooperative tone for the conversation. It reminds you both that alignment already exists in some areas, which can make it easier to address differences constructively.

- Example:
    - "I love that we both value Communication—it explains why we've been able to work through challenges in the past."
    - "It's great that Health is important to both of us. It shows that we both care about taking care of ourselves."

Why it works: Acknowledging alignment helps build trust and encourages both partners to feel heard and validated. It puts you

Nick Brancato

in a positive mindset to approach misalignments with openness rather than defensiveness.

2. Use "I" Statements to Avoid Blame

When discussing differences in priorities, it's essential to express your feelings without placing blame. Using "I" statements allows you to communicate your emotions and needs without making your partner feel attacked. This approach encourages empathy and understanding by focusing on your own experience, rather than assigning fault.

- Example:
    o "I feel more connected when we spend time with family, and I'd love to do that more often."
    o Compare this with: "You never make time for my family."

Why it works: When you own your feelings with "I" statements, your partner is more likely to listen without becoming defensive. It creates space for honest communication and fosters a collaborative atmosphere.

3. Ask Open-Ended Questions

When addressing areas of misalignment, it's important to explore your partner's perspective with open-ended questions. This allows you to understand the deeper motivations behind their priorities and avoid making assumptions. Open-ended questions encourage dialogue and help both partners feel respected and understood.

- Example:
  - "What makes Career a top priority for you right now?"
  - "What do you enjoy most about spending time with your friends?"

Why it works: Open-ended questions help uncover the underlying values behind your partner's actions and decisions. They allow you to dig deeper into what's driving their priorities and foster mutual empathy.

4. Look for Opportunities to Blend Priorities

Instead of viewing differences as obstacles, approach them as opportunities to blend your priorities in ways that honor both partners' values. The goal isn't to sacrifice one person's needs for the other's, but to find creative solutions that satisfy both.

- Example:
  - If one partner values Health and the other prioritizes Entertainment, try going on a fun hike or bike ride together—combining exercise with leisure.
  - If one partner prioritizes Career and the other Relationships, plan a work-free date night each week to maintain balance.

Why it works: Blending priorities helps both partners feel seen and valued, fostering a sense of teamwork. It also reduces the chance of resentment by ensuring that both partners' needs are incorporated into shared decisions.

5. Create an Action Plan Together

Use the insights from your conversation to set small, achievable goals that reflect both partners' values. An action plan provides clarity on how you'll balance priorities and creates accountability for following through. The plan doesn't have to be complicated—small changes can have a big impact over time.

- Example:
    - "Let's agree to limit work emails on the weekend, so we can enjoy quality time together."
    - "We'll set a travel budget each month, so we can still have adventures while saving for the future."

Why it works: Creating an action plan ensures that both partners are actively participating in finding solutions. It turns your insights into practical steps, keeping your conversations from becoming abstract or stagnant.

6. Revisit the Test Periodically

Your priorities—and your relationship—will evolve over time. That's why it's essential to revisit the Prioritize Us Test at least every 6 to 12 months. This allows you to reflect on any changes in your values or circumstances and adjust your action plan accordingly. Life transitions, such as a new job, having children, or health challenges, can shift what feels most important. Regular check-ins help your relationship stay intentional and adaptable.

- Example:
    - "It's been a few months since we took the test—do you feel like any of your priorities have shifted?"

o "Let's see if there are any new areas we need to align now that we've started this new phase in life."

Why it works: Revisiting the test ensures that your relationship stays in tune with your evolving priorities. It helps prevent future misalignment by encouraging regular communication and intentional adjustments.

Couple Case Study: Ben and Mia's TDS of 34

Ben and Mia have been together for three years, and while they love each other deeply, they've noticed an increasing number of arguments—especially about how they spend their time and money. Mia felt that Ben was too focused on his career and wasn't making enough time for them to connect. On the other hand, Ben felt frustrated with Mia's spending on travel and social events, believing it was reckless. These disagreements were slowly eroding their connection, leaving both partners feeling unheard, misunderstood, and disconnected.

To better understand the root of their tension, they decided to take the Prioritize Us Test. They hoped it would provide clarity about their values and offer insights into why these conflicts kept recurring.

Ben and Mia's Test Results: A Snapshot of Their Priorities

Priority	Ben's Rank	Mia's Rank	Difference
Career	2	7	5
Communication	4	3	1

Entertainment	9	5	4
Finances	1	6	5
Growth	6	4	2
Health	5	2	3
Relationships	8	1	7
Safety	3	8	5
Sex	7	9	2
Spirituality	10	10	0

Total Difference Score (TDS): 34

Insights from Ben and Mia's TDS of 34

When Ben and Mia reviewed their TDS of 34, they realized that most of their misalignment stemmed from differences in how they valued time and money. Ben ranked Career and Finances as top priorities, while Mia placed higher importance on Relationships and Entertainment. These differences had become the source of ongoing conflict, but the test helped them view their situation more clearly —and with more empathy.

Key Misalignments and New Understandings

1. Career vs. Relationships

- **The Conflict:** Mia felt that Ben was too focused on his career, interpreting his long work hours as a lack of interest in spending time together.

86

- **The Insight:** After seeing the test results, Mia understood that Ben's focus on work wasn't about avoiding her—it reflected his desire to build financial security for their future. For Ben, his career wasn't just a job—it was how he showed his commitment to their life together.
- **The Resolution:** They agreed to schedule intentional time together every week—even during busy periods. This way, Mia could feel connected and valued, and Ben could focus on his work without guilt.

2. Finances vs. Entertainment and Experiences

- **The Conflict:** Ben believed Mia's spending on travel and social events was frivolous and clashed with his focus on saving for the future. He felt stressed by their lack of financial boundaries.
- **The Insight:** Through the test, Ben realized that Mia wasn't being careless—she valued experiences, relationships, and making memories with the people she loved. For Mia, spending on travel and social events was a way to nurture her relationships, which she saw as essential to her happiness.
- **The Resolution:** They agreed to create a travel budget that allowed Mia to enjoy experiences without compromising their savings goals. This gave Ben the financial structure he needed to feel secure, while Mia still had room to pursue her passions.

3. Safety vs. Flexibility

- **The Conflict:** Ben prioritized Safety much higher than Mia. For Ben, safety meant financial planning and predictability, while Mia was more comfortable with flexibility and spontaneity. This difference created tension around decision-making—Ben wanted to be cautious, while Mia preferred to embrace opportunities as they came.

- **The Insight:** By discussing their priorities, they began to understand that neither approach was right or wrong. Ben's focus on safety gave them stability, while Mia's spontaneity brought joy and adventure into their lives.
- **The Resolution:** They agreed to balance safety with flexibility—setting aside money for savings while also designating a portion for spontaneous experiences. This way, both partners could feel their needs were respected.

Areas of Alignment: Communication and Spirituality

In addition to identifying their differences, Ben and Mia also found areas where their priorities were well-aligned.

- **Communication:** Both partners ranked Communication highly, showing that they valued open dialogue and emotional connection. This shared value helped them resolve conflicts quickly once they started discussing their priorities.
- **Spirituality:** Neither Ben nor Mia placed a high value on Spirituality, which meant it wasn't a source of tension in their relationship. While they didn't engage in religious or spiritual practices, they respected each other's beliefs and didn't feel pressure to align in this area.

These aligned priorities served as strengths in their relationship, giving them common ground to build on.

The Impact of the Test: A Shift Toward Understanding and Balance

Taking the Prioritize Us Test gave Ben and Mia the tools to understand their differences without judgment. Before the test, Mia had felt neglected and frustrated by Ben's focus on work, while Ben felt stressed by Mia's spending habits. These misaligned priorities had been fueling arguments and causing emotional distance between them.

However, once they saw their priorities laid out clearly, they were able to reframe their frustrations. Instead of viewing each other's behavior as problematic, they began to see the deeper values driving those actions. This shift allowed them to communicate more effectively and collaborate on solutions that respected both partners' needs.

Moving Forward: Intentional Alignment in Their Relationship

With their new insights, Ben and Mia decided to make small but meaningful changes to align their priorities:

- **Weekly Quality Time:** They committed to setting aside one night each week for intentional connection, ensuring that Mia felt emotionally supported, even during Ben's busy work periods.
- **Travel Budget:** They created a budget for travel and social events that allowed Mia to enjoy meaningful experiences without causing Ben stress about finances.
- **Balancing Structure and Flexibility:** They agreed to balance financial security with spontaneity by setting aside savings but also leaving room for occasional, unplanned adventures.

89

Nick Brancato

These adjustments weren't about changing who they were—they were about finding ways to support each other's priorities intentionally.

Key Takeaways from Ben and Mia's Story

Ben and Mia's experience highlights how misaligned priorities can cause conflict if they go unacknowledged, but it also shows the power of understanding and collaboration. By taking the time to explore their values and priorities through the Prioritize Us Test, they were able to bridge the gaps between them and build a stronger, more intentional relationship.

Lessons from Ben and Mia:

1. Misalignment is natural—it's not about eliminating differences but about learning to balance and respect each other's priorities.
2. Open communication is essential—understanding what drives your partner's actions reduces frustration and builds empathy.
3. Small adjustments create big results—you don't need to change everything to see meaningful improvement. Intentional compromises can make a lasting difference.

By recognizing their differences, celebrating their strengths, and working together toward intentional alignment, Ben and Mia were able to turn conflict into connection—and build a relationship that reflects both their individual values and shared goals.

The Goal: Intentional Balance, Not Perfect Alignment

One of the most important takeaways from this process is that the goal of alignment isn't to eliminate differences. Every couple will have unique priorities—some that align naturally and others that don't. Differences are inevitable, but they don't have to create division. In fact, differences in priorities can enrich your relationship by bringing in diverse perspectives and new ways of thinking.

The key is to understand and respect these differences and work toward an intentional balance. When both partners feel seen, heard, and supported, they are more willing to collaborate on decisions that honor both sets of values. This creates a relationship where each person can thrive—not just as a partner but as an individual.

What's Next: Interpreting Your TDS Score

In the next chapter, we'll dive deeper into how to interpret your Total Difference Score (TDS) and what it reveals about your relationship dynamics. Whether your score is low, moderate, or high, every couple can use these insights to build greater alignment and strengthen their connection. A low score might indicate that you already align well, but there may still be opportunities for fine-tuning priorities. A high score isn't a sign of incompatibility—it's an invitation to grow through open conversations and intentional actions.

Regardless of your TDS, this process is about building a relationship that evolves with both of you. When you make alignment an ongoing practice, you create a relationship where both partners feel empowered to express their values, navigate differences with care, and grow together over time.

CHAPTER 5

Interpreting the Total Difference Score (TDS)

Understanding Your Total Difference Score (TDS)

The Total Difference Score (TDS) is more than just a number—it's a powerful tool for understanding the unique dynamics of your relationship. It offers insight into how your priorities align, where they diverge, and where tensions may arise. Whether your TDS is low, moderate, or high, the score helps you identify both strengths and challenges in your relationship, guiding you toward intentional conversations and thoughtful decisions.

The goal isn't to achieve a perfect TDS (spoiler: that's nearly impossible!). Even couples with strong, healthy relationships will have differences in priorities—it's a natural part of being two unique individuals. The real value of the TDS lies in what you do with the information. It's a starting point for deeper conversations and a guide for balancing your values intentionally, ensuring that both partners feel understood and supported.

How to Interpret Your TDS Score: What It Means for Your Relationship

Your TDS score falls into one of three categories: low, moderate, or high. Each score reflects a different dynamic in the relationship—not better or worse, just different. Let's explore what each range means and how to use those insights effectively.

1. Low TDS (0-10): Strong Alignment

A low TDS suggests that you and your partner have naturally aligned priorities. You share many of the same values, which makes it easier to navigate decisions and find common ground without much conflict.

- What this means:
    o You likely feel connected and understood in many areas of your relationship.
    o You probably make decisions—like how to spend time or money—without much tension.
    o Conversations about priorities may feel natural and easy.
- Potential Challenges:
    o Even with strong alignment, it's important to avoid complacency. Over time, individual priorities can shift, and if you aren't paying attention, these small changes can create new tensions.
    o Be mindful of areas where you might assume alignment but haven't discussed things explicitly.
    o There could be hidden differences that surface unexpectedly.
- Actionable Advice:
    o Celebrate your shared values and discuss how they strengthen your relationship.

93

o   Check in periodically to confirm that both of you still feel aligned, especially during life transitions (like new jobs, moving, or parenthood).

2. Moderate TDS (11-25): Balanced Misalignment

A moderate TDS indicates that you and your partner have some alignment in your priorities but also a few areas where your values differ significantly. This range is common for many couples and represents a healthy balance of similarities and differences.

- **What this means:**
    - o   Some areas of your relationship likely feel smooth, while others may require more intentional effort to navigate.
    - o   You might experience periodic disagreements— especially around the areas where your priorities diverge.
    - o   These differences aren't necessarily a problem but will require open communication and collaboration to balance effectively.
- **Potential Challenges:**
    - o   Without intentional alignment, small differences can escalate into recurring conflicts.
    - o   There's a risk of misinterpreting your partner's actions—for example, viewing their focus on work as neglect, when it's driven by a desire for financial security.
    - o   Some areas might require compromise—and if those conversations aren't managed well, one or both partners could feel unheard or unsupported.

- Actionable Advice:
    - Use the TDS as a conversation starter to explore your differing priorities without judgment.
    - Blend priorities intentionally by finding creative solutions that honor both partners' needs. For example, if one partner prioritizes growth and the other values stability, you might schedule adventure days within an otherwise structured routine.
    - Revisit the test every few months to track how your priorities evolve and adjust your action plan as needed.

3. High TDS (26+): Significant Misalignment

A high TDS suggests that you and your partner have significant differences in how you prioritize different areas of life. These differences may have already led to ongoing tension or misunderstandings, or they could represent areas of potential conflict if not addressed intentionally.

- What this means:
    - You likely approach life decisions from different perspectives, which may make some conversations more challenging.
    - It's possible that one or both partners feel misunderstood or unappreciated for their efforts.
    - The misalignment doesn't mean the relationship is doomed—it simply highlights areas where greater empathy, compromise, and intentional alignment are needed.
- Potential Challenges:

- o If these differences go unaddressed, they can lead to resentment or emotional distance.
- o Partners might fall into a pattern of blame—for example, criticizing each other for how they spend time or money, without understanding the underlying values driving those choices.
- o A high TDS may require more effort and communication to ensure that both partners feel valued and supported.
- **Actionable Advice:**
  - o Approach conversations with curiosity rather than criticism—try to understand why certain priorities matter to your partner.
  - o Set realistic goals for alignment. You don't have to agree on everything, but you can find ways to support each other's priorities intentionally.
  - o Consider blending or alternating priorities—for example, one weekend could focus on career tasks while the next is reserved for quality time with family.
  - o If ongoing tension persists, you might benefit from relationship coaching or therapy to help navigate more complex misalignments.

How to Use Your TDS as a Tool for Growth

Regardless of your TDS score, the insights you gain from the Prioritize Us Test are an opportunity to grow closer as a couple. The score is not a measure of your relationship's success—it's a roadmap for deeper conversations and more intentional decision-making.

Here are some practical ways to use your TDS for growth:

1. Turn Differences into Conversations:

- Use your TDS to explore misaligned priorities without judgment. Ask open-ended questions to understand why your partner values certain things.

2. Celebrate Your Strengths:

- Identify and celebrate the areas of alignment—these are the strengths that can anchor your relationship.

3. Create an Action Plan:

- Develop a plan to blend or balance priorities that differ. This might involve setting boundaries around work time, budgeting for both savings and experiences, or scheduling intentional time for connection.

4. Revisit the Test Periodically:

- Life changes, and so do priorities. Make it a habit to revisit the test at least every 6 to 12 months to ensure your relationship stays aligned and adapts to new circumstances.

A Tool for Intentional Alignment

Your TDS score isn't the final word on your relationship—it's a starting point for growth. Whether your score is low, moderate, or high, it provides valuable insights into the unique dynamics between you and your partner. The goal isn't to achieve perfect alignment but to understand each other's priorities and work together intentionally to balance them.

Nick Brancato

By using the TDS as a guide for conversations, empathy, and collaboration, you'll build a relationship that feels authentic and fulfilling—one that reflects both your individual values and your shared vision for the future.

The Couples Compatibility Continuum: From Symbiotic to Polarized

The Couples Compatibility Continuum provides a framework for interpreting your Total Difference Score (TDS). The TDS ranges from 0 to 50, reflecting the total difference between how you and your partner rank your top 10 priorities. A low score suggests that your priorities are closely aligned, while a higher score indicates greater differences that may require intentional conversations and compromise.

This continuum isn't about labeling relationships as "good" or "bad"—it's about providing clarity. Each point on the continuum offers insights into how much effort or adjustment may be needed to create balance and connection in your relationship. No matter where you fall on the scale, alignment is always within reach if both partners are committed to open communication and intentional growth.

Understanding the Compatibility Continuum

Below is a breakdown of the TDS ranges, including what each score means for your relationship and how it can guide your next steps toward alignment.

TDS Score	Compatibility Label	What It Means
0	Symbiotic	Perfect alignment. Your priorities are fully in sync—an extremely

		rare occurrence. Your relationship reflects near-total harmony, with both partners naturally aligned in their values and decisions.
1-5	Synchronized	Strong alignment with only minor differences. Maintaining harmony requires little effort, and any adjustments needed are easy and natural. This range suggests your relationship runs smoothly without significant tension.
6-10	Harmonized	Your priorities are mostly aligned, with a few small gaps that may require occasional adjustments. You likely experience minor disagreements, but alignment feels natural and easy to maintain.
11-15	Unified	Moderate alignment. You share many values, but a few key differences will require intentional conversations to stay balanced. With open communication, you can maintain connection and

		address small misalignments as they arise.
16-20	Coordinated	Some misalignment. Regular discussions and compromises are needed to stay connected. You and your partner likely view certain priorities differently, and without intentional balancing, these differences could cause tension over time.
21-25	Complementary	Different but compatible. You and your partner may have contrasting priorities, but with empathy, respect, and active balancing, these differences can complement each other. Alignment will require consistent effort to ensure both partners feel supported.
26-30	Divergent	Significant differences in how you prioritize life's key areas. Ongoing conversations are essential to prevent unresolved tension from building. Without effort, these differences

		could strain your connection over time.
31-35	Contrasting	Major misalignment. Your values and priorities differ in several key areas, and deeper work is required to reconcile your differences. Intentional alignment will take effort, and it may be necessary to restructure routines or goals to create balance.
36-40	Fragmented	Serious misalignment. You and your partner may struggle to find common ground, with significant differences impacting how you spend time, manage money, or connect emotionally. Regular communication and deliberate compromise are critical to maintaining your relationship.
41-50	Polarized	Critical misalignment. Your priorities are deeply at odds, and it may feel like you're living on different pages. Professional guidance, such as couples therapy or

		coaching, can provide tools to help you navigate these deep seated differences and find paths toward alignment.

Using the Compatibility Continuum to Strengthen Your Relationship

No matter where you and your partner fall on the TDS scale, alignment is always achievable with intentional effort and open communication. Each range on the continuum offers unique opportunities for growth. Even couples with higher TDS scores can thrive if they approach their differences with curiosity, empathy, and collaboration. Below are a few strategies based on your TDS range to help you turn insights into action.

Strategies Based on Your TDS Score

0-10: Symbiotic, Synchronized, or Harmonized (Low TDS)

- **Focus on Maintenance:** Since your priorities are already well-aligned, focus on maintaining this harmony by checking in periodically to ensure your values remain in sync.
- **Celebrate Your Strengths:** Use this opportunity to strengthen your relationship even further by building on your shared values. For example, if Health is a top priority for both of you, create new wellness goals together.

11-25: Unified, Coordinated, or Complementary (Moderate TDS)

- **Open Conversations are Key:** While you're fairly aligned, a few differences may need ongoing attention to maintain balance. Have regular check-ins to discuss where your priorities are shifting and where compromises may be needed.
- **Blend Your Priorities:** Find ways to integrate each partner's priorities. For example, if one of you prioritizes work and the other values relationships, schedule weekly date nights that fit around busy work hours.

26-35: Divergent, or Contrasting (High TDS)

- **Prioritize Empathy and Compromise:** This range suggests that your priorities may pull you in different directions at times. Focus on empathizing with each other's perspectives and actively balancing your needs.
- **Create a Structured Action Plan:** Set small, actionable goals that address specific areas of misalignment. For example, if one partner prioritizes saving money while the other values experiences, agree to allocate part of your budget toward both savings and travel.

36-50: Fragmented, or Polarized (Very High TDS)

- **Build Trust Through Conversations:** In this range, significant misalignments may cause frustration or emotional distance. Start with non-judgmental conversations to understand the deeper values driving each partner's actions.

- **Consider Professional Support:** If you feel stuck or overwhelmed by the differences, couples therapy or coaching can provide guidance and tools to help you navigate complex misalignments.
- **Focus on Small Wins:** Instead of trying to align everything at once, focus on small areas of progress to build momentum. Celebrating these wins can restore trust and strengthen your connection over time.

The TDS as a Tool for Ongoing Growth

Your TDS score is not a fixed label—it's a snapshot of where your relationship stands right now. As life evolves, so will your priorities, which means your TDS may shift over time. Regularly revisiting the Prioritize Us Test helps you stay in tune with your partner's values and ensure that your relationship remains intentional and adaptable.

By acknowledging differences without judgment and finding creative ways to align, you can use your TDS as a roadmap for growth. Whether your score is low or high, the insights from the test offer you the tools to build a stronger, more balanced relationship—one that reflects both partners' individual identities and shared vision for the future.

What Your TDS Reveals

Now that you know where your relationship falls on the Total Difference Score (TDS) scale, let's explore what your score actually means. Whether your TDS is low, moderate, or high, it provides valuable insights into both the strengths and growth opportunities in your relationship. Your score isn't a judgment—it's a guide for understanding where you're aligned and where you'll need to be more intentional in balancing priorities.

Each TDS range reflects how much effort may be required to maintain or strengthen alignment. Regardless of where you fall on the scale, with curiosity, empathy, and communication, you can create a relationship that supports both your individual values and your shared goals.

Low TDS (0–10): Strong Alignment

A low TDS indicates that your priorities are well-aligned, creating a natural sense of harmony in your relationship. Decision-making tends to feel easy, and you likely experience minimal conflict about how you allocate time, money, and energy. While you're in a great place, it's important to remember that life changes—such as career shifts, family responsibilities, or personal growth—can cause priorities to shift over time.

Symbiotic (0)

- "Are you soulmates, or did you just read each other's minds?"
  - o A score of 0 means your priorities are perfectly aligned—an incredibly rare occurrence. You share an almost identical perspective on what matters most in life, which minimizes tension and promotes natural, effortless connection.
- What to watch for:
  - o Even with perfect alignment now, life events can shift priorities over time. Be sure to have regular check-ins to ensure you stay connected and aware of any new changes.

Synchronized (1–5)

- "Minor differences, but mostly smooth sailing."
  - o Your relationship is marked by strong alignment, with only a few small differences in your priorities. Conversations about what matters come naturally, and you likely experience very little conflict when making decisions together.
- What to watch for:
  - o Keep an eye on life changes—a new job, moving to a new city, or shifting family goals could introduce subtle misalignments.

Harmonized (6–10)

- "Mostly aligned, with a few minor bumps along the way."
  - o Your relationship shows strong alignment overall, with just a few areas where your priorities differ slightly. These small gaps may cause occasional disagreements, but they're relatively easy to resolve through light, intentional conversations.
- What to watch for:
  - o As long as you're willing to discuss minor differences openly, staying aligned will feel natural and manageable over time.

Moderate TDS (11–25): Room for Adjustment

A moderate TDS means that you and your partner share many values, but some key differences exist that could lead to tension if left unaddressed. You'll need to pay attention to these gaps and have regular conversations to keep your priorities aligned as life evolves.

Unified (11–15)

- "Aligned with a few important differences."
  - o You have a solid foundation in your relationship, but some differences in priorities may surface around time, money, or energy. These gaps can be managed with small compromises and intentional effort to stay aligned.
- What to watch for:
  - o Keep communication open, especially during life transitions, and check in regularly to ensure that both partners feel seen and supported.

Coordinated (16–20)

- "Mostly in sync, but some differences require effort to manage."
  - o You're aligned in many areas, but some significant differences may require ongoing discussions and adjustments. These differences could create tension over time if not handled intentionally.
- What to watch for:
  - o Stay curious about your partner's perspective— understanding their deeper motivations can help you avoid misunderstandings and prevent friction.

Complementary (21–25)

- "Different, but not incompatible."
  - o Your priorities diverge, but with respect and active balancing, these differences can work in your favor. By honoring each other's values, you can

prevent conflict and find ways to blend your priorities into a cohesive partnership.

- What to watch for:
  - o Schedule regular check-ins to ensure both partners feel valued and understood, especially in areas where your priorities differ

High TDS (26–35): Requires Intentional Alignment

A high TDS indicates that you and your partner have noticeable differences in your values and priorities. These differences aren't insurmountable, but they will require regular, intentional conversations to prevent misunderstandings and keep the relationship balanced. With effort, your differences can even become complementary strengths.

Divergent (26–30)

- "Significant differences—intentional effort required."
  - o You and your partner have notable differences in how you prioritize time, money, or energy.
  - o Without intentional conversations, these differences could lead to tension and disconnect over time.
- What to watch for:
  - o Be proactive in addressing conflicting values to avoid misunderstandings. Use empathy and open communication to bridge the gaps between your priorities.

Contrasting (31–35)

- "Major misalignments that need deeper work."
    - o Your relationship contains significant misalignments, and without active effort, these differences could lead to ongoing tension. It will take intentional compromises and frequent discussions to maintain connection and avoid friction.
- What to watch for:
    - o You may need to restructure some routines or habits to accommodate both partners' values.

Very High TDS (36–50): Critical Misalignment

A very high TDS reflects serious differences between you and your partner's priorities. These misalignments are likely causing persistent tension or misunderstandings. While these differences may feel overwhelming, alignment is still possible with open conversations, empathy, and, in some cases, professional support.

Fragmented (36–40)

- "Serious misalignment, with regular tension."
    - o Your priorities are frequently in conflict, and you may experience ongoing frustration or misunderstandings. Finding common ground will require open, honest conversations and significant compromise.
- What to watch for:
    - o Focus on small wins—address one area at a time to rebuild trust and restore connection.

Polarized (41–50)

- "Living on different pages—professional guidance recommended."
    - o ∘   A TDS in this range suggests deep, persistent misalignment. You and your partner may feel like you're living on different planets, with very little common ground. Without intervention, these differences could lead to ongoing conflict or emotional distance.
- What to watch for:
    - o Consider working with a relationship coach or therapist to help bridge the gaps and develop tools for better alignment.

The TDS as a Roadmap for Growth

No matter where your relationship falls on the TDS scale, the score provides a roadmap for understanding and growth. Whether your priorities are mostly aligned or significantly misaligned, the key to building a healthy relationship is communication, empathy, and intentional alignment.

Alignment isn't about achieving perfection—it's about understanding each other's values and finding ways to balance both partners' needs. With the insights from your TDS, you have everything you need to start meaningful conversations, create actionable plans, and build a relationship that reflects both individual values and shared goals.

Probability Insights: Perfect Alignment Is Rare, and That's Okay

It's easy to feel discouraged when you see a high TDS score—but it's important to understand that misalignment is completely normal. In fact, achieving perfect alignment (a TDS of 0) is so rare that the odds are 1 in 13 trillion.

That means it's virtually impossible for two people to have identical priorities across every area of life. Differences are not a sign of failure—they're a natural part of being in a relationship. The goal isn't perfection but rather understanding, balancing, and aligning your values intentionally over time.

Let's dive into some key insights about TDS scores and what they reveal about the dynamics of most relationships.

Fascinating Insights About TDS Scores

1. Most Couples Score Between 11–25 on the TDS Scale

- The 11–25 range is the most common range for couples, representing moderate differences in values. In this range, partners share many priorities, but small misalignments start to appear— such as disagreements about time management, finances, or social activities.
- Why this matters:
  - These small gaps are normal and can be addressed with open conversations. In fact, working through these differences often strengthens the relationship by building empathy and understanding.

2. Less Than 1% of Couples Score Below 5

- Scores below 5 indicate near-perfect alignment—a very rare occurrence. These couples often share similar life goals, worldviews, or cultural backgrounds, making it easier to navigate priorities without conflict.
- Why this matters:
  - While near-perfect alignment can feel effortless, these couples aren't immune to life's challenges. Priorities can shift over time, and even highly aligned couples will need to adapt as circumstances change.

3. High TDS Scores (30+) Are Common During Life Transitions

- TDS scores above 30 aren't uncommon among couples going through major life transitions, such as becoming parents, managing career shifts, or moving to a new city. During these periods, partners may experience temporary misalignment as they adapt to new roles, responsibilities, or expectations.
- Why this matters:
  - These transitional phases offer an opportunity for growth and realignment. With intentional conversations and empathy, partners can rediscover balance and strengthen their connection through change.

Your TDS Is Just a Snapshot—Not a Measure of Love

One of the most important things to remember is that your TDS score isn't a reflection of how much you love each other. It's simply a snapshot of how your priorities align at this moment in time. Every couple—no matter how aligned—will experience shifts in priorities throughout the course of their relationship. Alignment isn't static; it's a process that requires regular check-ins, empathy, and small adjustments along the way.

For couples with lower TDS scores: Celebrate your alignment, but stay mindful of life's inevitable changes. Regular communication will help you stay connected and in sync as new priorities arise.

For couples with higher TDS scores: View misalignment as an opportunity for growth, not a problem. Differences are natural, and addressing them together can deepen your connection and lead to creative solutions that honor both partners' needs.

The Key Takeaway: Alignment Is Always Within Reach

No matter what your TDS score reveals, alignment is always possible if both partners are willing to engage in open conversations. The beauty of intentional alignment is that it's not about achieving perfection—it's about growing together over time. Every conversation about your priorities, every compromise, and every small adjustment brings you closer to a relationship where both partners feel seen, heard, and supported.

So, take heart—your score is not a verdict but an invitation. Whether you're starting from a place of strong alignment or working through misalignment, you and your partner have the opportunity to build the kind of relationship that reflects your evolving values and shared vision.

Small Steps, Big Impact

Creating alignment in your relationship doesn't require major, sweeping changes—it's the small, intentional actions that make the biggest difference. Whether that means adjusting routines, setting new boundaries, or finding creative ways to blend priorities, every small step contributes to building a relationship where both partners feel heard, valued, and supported.

For example:

- Scheduling regular check-ins to reflect on how your priorities are evolving.
- Setting shared goals—like balancing career ambitions with quality time or budgeting for both savings and experiences.
- Making space for both individuality and togetherness, ensuring that each partner feels free to pursue personal interests while nurturing the relationship.

These small actions accumulate over time, creating momentum and connection that carries you through inevitable changes and challenges.

Navigating the Ups and Downs Together

Every couple will encounter moments of misalignment, and that's okay. These moments are not signs of failure—they are opportunities for growth. Misalignment can reveal deeper values that weren't previously discussed, giving you both a chance to recalibrate and understand each other better. The key is to approach differences with empathy and curiosity instead of frustration or judgment.

You're not on opposite sides of a problem—you're partners working together to build a life that reflects both of your values. When you learn to navigate misalignments constructively, you create a relationship that is flexible, resilient, and adaptable to life's inevitable changes.

Looking Ahead: Practical Tools for Navigating Conflict Zones

Your TDS offers a roadmap for understanding where your strengths and growth opportunities lie. The next step is learning how to apply those insights to real-life situations. In the upcoming chapter, we'll dive into the most common areas of conflict that arise from misaligned priorities—such as time management, finances, intimacy, and personal growth.

You'll discover practical strategies to navigate these conflict zones effectively and build healthy communication patterns that bring you closer. Whether you're dealing with minor disagreements or deeper tensions, these tools will help you collaborate as a team and keep your relationship aligned with what matters most.

Choose Alignment, One Step at a Time

Alignment is an ongoing choice—a process of showing up for each other intentionally, even when life gets busy or complicated. Your relationship will evolve, and so will your priorities. With awareness, empathy, and open communication, you can navigate these changes with confidence and build a partnership that reflects both your individual growth and your shared vision for the future.

Wherever your TDS score places you today, remember that alignment is always within reach—one conversation, one compromise, and one intentional action at a time. Let's continue the path toward a more connected, balanced, and intentional relationship.

CHAPTER 6

Conflict Zones—Where Priorities Collide

Even the most aligned couples experience conflict from time to time, especially when their priorities collide in key areas. These moments of tension can feel overwhelming, but they are also opportunities for growth. The goal isn't to avoid conflict entirely—it's to learn how to navigate disagreements in ways that strengthen your relationship and bring greater alignment over time.

In this chapter, we'll explore which priorities are most likely to create conflict, provide communication tools and conflict resolution strategies, and share a case study of a couple overcoming their differences. You'll also find a conflict management exercise at the end of the chapter to help you apply these strategies to your relationship.

Identifying Key Conflict Areas

Some priorities are more prone to cause conflict than others because they impact core aspects of daily life—how you spend your time, money, and emotional energy. These areas often become flashpoints for disagreement and misunderstanding because they touch on deeply held beliefs about safety, connection, achievement, and fulfillment. When left unresolved, conflicts in these areas can create emotional distance, resentment, and frustration. But when addressed with empathy and intention, they provide opportunities for growth, deeper understanding, and alignment.

Let's take a closer look at four common conflict zones, why they tend to cause tension, and how they can impact your relationship.

1. Finances: Balancing Security and Enjoyment

Money is one of the most common sources of conflict in relationships, but disagreements about finances are rarely just about dollars and cents. For many people, money represents more than its face value—it can symbolize security, freedom, status, or fulfillment. Partners often differ in how they view financial decisions, with one emphasizing long-term planning and the other focusing on enjoying life in the present. These differing mindsets can lead to misunderstandings and tension if not openly discussed.

- **Common Conflict:**
    - One partner prioritizes saving for the future (such as retirement or buying a home), while the other prefers to spend on experiences, like travel, dining out, or hobbies.
    - **Impact:** The saver may feel that their partner's spending is reckless, while the spender may feel stifled or deprived, leading to resentment on both sides.

How It Impacts the Relationship:

- Disagreements over budgeting and spending priorities can create tension, especially if one partner feels that the other is not valuing financial security or, conversely, not allowing room for joy. Without open discussions, these differences can erode trust and lead to feelings of being misunderstood or even financial anxiety.

2. Communication: Navigating Different Styles and Needs

Communication styles can differ greatly between partners, leading to frustration when one person's needs for connection don't align with the other's. While some people thrive on daily emotional checkins, others prefer brief, functional conversations and need more personal space to recharge. When these differences go unaddressed, partners may feel unheard or disconnected, creating unnecessary tension.

- **Common Conflict:**
  - One partner feels connected through frequent emotional check-ins and deep conversations, while the other finds these interactions overwhelming and prefers more space or light, practical exchanges.
  - **Impact:** The emotionally expressive partner may feel neglected or dismissed, while the more reserved partner may feel pressured or criticized for not communicating enough.

How It Impacts the Relationship:

- Communication breakdowns can cause misunderstandings about each partner's emotional needs. If one person craves consistent dialogue but the other prefers minimal interaction, both partners can feel frustrated. Over time, these differences may lead to emotional distance or leave one partner feeling unappreciated for their efforts to connect.

3. Career vs. Relationships: Balancing Ambition and Connection

A common tension in relationships arises when partners have different views on the balance between career and personal life. One partner may be career-driven, seeing their work as a path to achievement, fulfillment, or financial stability. The other may feel that time together is more important and prioritize quality time over professional ambitions. When these priorities clash, both partners may end up feeling unheard, misunderstood, or unappreciated.

- **Common Conflict:**
  - One partner works long hours to pursue career goals, believing that their hard work benefits the relationship in the long run. Meanwhile, the other partner feels neglected and wishes for more time and connection.
  - **Impact:** The partner focusing on career may feel unsupported or unfairly criticized, while the other partner feels emotionally abandoned and questions whether they are a priority.

How It Impacts the Relationship:

- Tensions between work and personal life can create a sense of imbalance in the relationship. Without intentional efforts to align these priorities, both partners may feel frustrated and disconnected, leading to repeated arguments about how time is spent. Over time, unresolved tension in this area can cause resentment and erode trust.

4. Intimacy and Sex: Bridging Physical and Emotional Connection

Intimacy and sex are often complex areas in relationships, as partners may have different needs for physical and emotional connection. One partner might see frequent physical intimacy as a primary way of expressing love and feeling connected, while the other may prioritize emotional closeness over physical touch. These differences can lead to misunderstandings, unmet expectations, and hurt feelings if not openly addressed.

- Common Conflict:
    - o One partner may feel rejected or unwanted when physical intimacy needs aren't met, while the other may feel pressured or emotionally disconnected, making it hard to engage physically.
    - o **Impact:** The partner craving physical intimacy may internalize rejection, leading to frustration or insecurity, while the other partner may feel overwhelmed or criticized for not meeting those expectations.

How It Impacts the Relationship:

- Differences in intimacy needs can create a cycle of frustration and resentment, with one partner feeling unfulfilled and the other feeling pressured or misunderstood. If these needs aren't discussed with empathy and openness, they can lead to emotional distance and leave both partners feeling unseen and unappreciated.

The Power of Recognizing Common Conflict Zones

Recognizing these four key conflict areas—finances, communication, career vs. relationships, and intimacy—is the first step toward addressing them with empathy and intention. Many conflicts arise not because partners don't care about each other but because they prioritize different needs or express love and connection in different ways. These difference are natural but can create tension if they go unacknowledged.

By identifying these flashpoints early, couples can have open, constructive conversations before small disagreements turn into larger, ongoing conflicts. Understanding your partner's values and priorities allows you to bridge the gaps between you and create intentional alignment in your relationship.

Navigating Conflict Zones with Intention

Now that we've identified the most common areas of conflict, it's time to explore practical strategies for navigating them effectively. In the next section, we'll dive into tools and techniques for managing these differences, including how to:

- Blend priorities creatively to honor both partners' values.
- Communicate effectively without blame or frustration.
- Set boundaries and compromises that support both personal growth and relationship goals.
- Stay connected emotionally and physically, even when intimacy needs differ.

The goal isn't to eliminate conflict entirely—it's to navigate differences with empathy and build a relationship that reflects both your individual identities and shared goals. Let's explore how to turn conflict zones into opportunities for growth and strengthen your connection moving forward.

How to Navigate Conflict Zones Effectively

The goal in conflict isn't to win or prove a point—it's to gain a deeper understanding of your partner's perspective and work toward solutions that reflect both of your values. Conflict, when approached with empathy and intention, can become an opportunity for growth, alignment, and deeper connection. Differences don't have to divide you—instead, they can be bridges to greater understanding. Below are five key strategies to help you navigate conflict zones effectively and transform disagreements into opportunities for alignment.

1. Shift from Winning to Understanding

It's easy to fall into the trap of trying to convince your partner that your way of seeing things is the "right" way. But approaching conflict as a competition only creates distance. Instead, shift your mindset from winning to learning. Ask yourself: "What can I learn from my partner's perspective?" When you focus on understanding rather than being right, you create space for deeper conversations about why certain priorities matter to both of you.

- **Example:**
    - Instead of thinking, "How can I get them to see things my way?" try asking, "What values or experiences are shaping their perspective?"
    - If your partner prioritizes career growth, for example, try to understand what personal meaning their work holds—perhaps they see it as a way to provide security or feel fulfilled.

Why it works: This shift from judgment to curiosity reduces defensiveness and helps you appreciate your partner's values, even when you disagree. It builds empathy and makes it easier to find common ground.

2. Use "I" Statements to Avoid Blame

When conflict arises, it's important to communicate your feelings without assigning blame. Using "I" statements allows you to express yourself in a way that invites conversation rather than triggering defensiveness. Instead of saying, "You never..." or "You always...", focus on how specific actions make you feel and what you need moving forward.

- **Example:**
    - Instead of saying, "You never spend enough time with me," try: "I feel disconnected when we don't spend quality time together."
    - This shift focuses on your emotions rather than criticizing your partner, which keeps the conversation constructive.

Why it works: "I" statements foster open dialogue by focusing on your experience rather than blaming your partner. They also make it easier for your partner to hear and respond to your needs without becoming defensive.

3. Validate Your Partner's Experience

Validation is a powerful tool in conflict resolution. It doesn't mean you agree with everything your partner says—it simply means you acknowledge their feelings and experiences as real and valid. This act of recognition helps your partner feel seen and understood, even if you have different perspectives.

- Example:
    - If your partner wants to save more money while you prefer to spend on experiences, you could say: "I can see why saving is so important to you. It makes you feel secure and prepared for the future."

Why it works: Validation builds emotional safety, helping both partners feel heard and respected. When people feel validated, they're more likely to open up and engage in collaborative problem solving rather than becoming defensive.

4. Create Collaborative Solutions

The best resolutions honor both partners' priorities by finding win-win solutions. Instead of framing conflict as a matter of "either/or," look for ways to blend your priorities. This approach shows that you value both your partner's needs and your own, fostering mutual respect and deepening connection.

- **Example:**
  - o If one partner wants to save money and the other prioritizes entertainment, they could agree to a monthly date night with a set budget. This way, the saver feels financially responsible, and the other partner still gets to enjoy meaningful experiences.

Why it works: Collaborative solutions demonstrate that both partners are invested in the relationship's success. They help avoid resentment by ensuring that both individuals feel valued and that their needs are being taken seriously.

5. Take Breaks When Needed

Not every conflict can be resolved in one sitting. If a conversation becomes too heated or emotionally overwhelming, it's okay to pause and take a break. Agree on a specific time to revisit the discussion with fresh perspectives. Taking a break isn't avoidance—it's a way to regulate emotions and return to the conversation when both partners are calm and ready to engage productively.

- **Example:**
  - o If a discussion about finances escalates, you might say: "Let's take a break and come back to this in an hour. I want to make sure we have a calm conversation."

Why it works: Taking breaks allows both partners to cool down and reflect before continuing the discussion. It helps prevent escalation and ensures that the conversation stays productive and respectful.

Turning Conflict into Connection

Navigating conflict zones effectively isn't about eliminating disagreements—it's about learning from them and using them as opportunities to align your priorities intentionally. With the right strategies, you can reduce tension, build empathy, and deepen trust in your relationship.

By shifting from winning to understanding, using "I" statements, validating your partner's experience, creating collaborative solutions, and taking breaks when needed, you'll create a framework for healthy, respectful conflict resolution. Every disagreement becomes an opportunity to learn more about each other, strengthen your connection, and build a relationship that reflects both your individual values and shared goals.

In the next section, we'll explore examples of how couples have applied these strategies to navigate common conflict zones—proving that with intentional communication and empathy, even the most challenging disagreements can lead to greater alignment and connection.

Case Study: Emma and Alex Navigate Career vs. Relationships

Emma and Alex had been together for five years when conflicts over time management began to escalate. Emma was focused on advancing her career, putting in long hours at the office, attending networking events, and taking on extra projects. For her, this was an important period of professional growth, and she felt motivated to build momentum in her career. Meanwhile, Alex placed a high value on quality time and relationships. He wanted to spend more time with Emma and felt increasingly neglected by her busy schedule.

Nick Brancato

At first, their arguments followed a familiar pattern:

- Alex would express frustration that Emma was prioritizing work over their relationship.
- Emma would feel attacked for pursuing her career goals and feel unappreciated for the effort she was putting into their future.

Each argument left both partners feeling misunderstood. Alex felt rejected and questioned whether he was truly important to Emma, while Emma felt pressured to choose between her relationship and her career. Every conversation seemed to end in frustration without a clear resolution, and resentment began to build between them.

The Turning Point: Discovering Their TDS Score

When Emma and Alex took the Prioritize Us Test, their Total Difference Score (TDS) was 22, placing them in the Complementary range. This score revealed that while their priorities weren't identical, they weren't inherently incompatible either. Their differences had the potential to complement each other if they learned how to communicate more effectively and align their priorities intentionally. The test gave them a new framework to reframe their conflicts—not as personal attacks, but as natural differences in values that could be balanced with effort.

How They Resolved the Conflict

The first breakthrough came when Emma made an effort to validate Alex's feelings. Instead of becoming defensive, she acknowledged how her long work hours were affecting him

128

emotionally. This shift in communication helped reduce tension and opened the door for a more productive conversation.

- **Emma:** "I realize that when I stay late at work, it makes you feel like you're not important to me. I want you to know that's not how I feel—I just get caught up in work because it matters so much right now."

Alex, in turn, responded with curiosity rather than judgment. For the first time, he began to see Emma's dedication to her career not as a rejection of their relationship but as a reflection of how much professional success mattered to her.

- **Alex:** "I didn't realize how much pressure you're under to succeed at work. I can see how important it is to you, and I want to support that."

This moment of mutual empathy allowed both Emma and Alex to feel heard and respected. Instead of arguing about who was right or wrong, they started working together to create solutions that honored both of their priorities.

The Plan: Blending Their Priorities

Together, Emma and Alex came up with a plan that would help them balance Emma's career goals with Alex's need for quality time. They committed to small, actionable changes that would make both of them feel valued and supported.

1. Set Boundaries Around Work Hours

- Emma agreed to leave the office by 6 p.m. at least three nights a week, ensuring they had more time together during the evenings. This gave Alex the consistency he needed without compromising Emma's commitment to her career.

2. Schedule Intentional Time Together

- They created a weekly date night—an evening reserved for just the two of them, with no phones or work talk allowed. This allowed Alex to feel connected and ensured they were nurturing their relationship, even during busy weeks.

3. Use Sunday Evenings to Align Their Schedules

- They set aside time every Sunday evening to review their upcoming schedules and plan ahead. This helped them balance Emma's professional commitments with their personal goals, giving both partners more clarity about the week ahead.

The Outcome: Rebuilding Trust and Reducing Tension

These small but meaningful changes had an immediate impact on Emma and Alex's relationship. Alex no longer felt neglected because Emma's efforts to set boundaries and prioritize their time together showed him that he mattered. Emma, in turn, felt less guilty about pursuing her career because Alex expressed support for her ambitions and understood the pressure she was under.

- Trust was rebuilt as they honored their commitments to one another. Alex felt more secure, knowing that he could count on regular quality time, and Emma felt less stressed, knowing that her career goals were being supported rather than criticized.

- Their weekly date nights became a source of joy rather than an obligation. Without distractions from work, they could fully engage with each other, rekindling the connection that had felt strained by their busy schedules.
- The Sunday evening check-ins helped them stay on the same page. When unexpected changes came up—such as work events or family obligations—they could adjust proactively instead of reacting with frustration.

Ultimately, Emma and Alex were able to transform their conflict zone into a strength. Their

relationship became a source of support rather than stress, with each partner feeling more valued and understood.

Key Takeaways from Emma and Alex's Experience

1. Validation Builds Trust:

- Emma and Alex's breakthrough began when Emma validated Alex's feelings instead of dismissing his concerns. This simple act of acknowledgment opened the door for empathy and deeper understanding.

2. Curiosity Reduces Judgment:

- When Alex approached Emma with curiosity rather than criticism, it shifted the dynamic of their conversations. By seeking to understand her priorities, he made space for both of their values to coexist.

Nick Brancato

3. Small Changes Create Big Impact:

- Their solutions—such as setting work boundaries, scheduling date nights, and using Sunday check-ins— were small but powerful. These intentional adjustments reduced tension and helped them align their priorities over time.

4. Alignment is an Ongoing Process:

- Emma and Alex's experience highlights the importance of regular communication. Life will continue to bring new challenges, but with intentional check-ins, they are now equipped to adjust their priorities together.

Turning Conflict Into Connection

Emma and Alex's story shows that conflict doesn't have to divide you—it can bring you closer if approached with empathy, curiosity, and intentional action. Their TDS score of 22 indicated that while their priorities weren't identical, their differences were complementary—and with the right communication, they could find balance and alignment.

By validating each other's experiences, creating collaborative solutions, and making small but meaningful changes, they were able to reduce tension and rebuild trust. Their story is a reminder that even when your priorities differ, alignment is always possible with open conversations and intentional effort.

Every relationship will encounter moments of misalignment, but these moments are opportunities for growth. With the right tools and mindset, you can navigate conflict zones effectively and create a partnership where both partners feel seen, valued, and supported.

Exercise: Conflict Management and Reflection

This exercise is designed to help you reflect on recent conflicts in your relationship, understand the priorities at play, and work toward collaborative solutions. By taking the time to analyze your reactions and explore your partner's perspective, you'll gain the tools to navigate future conflicts more effectively.

Remember, the goal isn't to avoid conflict entirely—it's to approach disagreements with empathy and turn them into opportunities for growth and alignment.

1. Identify a Recent Conflict

Reflect on a disagreement you and your partner had recently. Take a few moments to write down the details of the conflict and identify the priorities that clashed.

- **What was the disagreement about?**
    - (Example: "We argued about whether to go to my family's dinner or attend a work event.")
- **Which priorities were in conflict?**
    - (Example: Relationships vs. Career. One of you prioritized family time, while the other wanted to attend a networking event to advance your career.)

Why this matters: Identifying the root priorities helps you move beyond surface-level disagreements and recognize the deeper values driving the conflict.

2. Reflect on Your Reactions

It's important to evaluate your own behavior during the conflict. Were you calm and open, or did you react defensively?

133

Understanding your emotional responses will help you respond more intentionally in the future.

- **How did you respond during the conflict?**
  - (Example: "I got frustrated and said things I didn't mean.")
- **How do you think your partner was feeling?**
  - (Example: "I think they felt hurt because they thought I didn't care about their career goals.")

Why this matters: Reflecting on your reactions helps you gain self-awareness about how you contribute to conflict. Recognizing your partner's emotions fosters empathy and encourages more productive conversations.

3. Explore Your Partner's Perspective

Take a moment to put yourself in your partner's shoes. Even if you didn't agree with their behavior, try to understand what value or priority might have been driving it. This shift in perspective can help you approach the conversation with curiosity instead of judgment.

- **What value or priority might have been driving your partner's behavior?**
  - (Example: "They prioritized their career because they're feeling pressure to succeed at work.")
- **How can you validate your partner's feelings without dismissing your own?**
  - (Example: "I can say, 'I understand that attending this work event is important to you, and I also value time with my family.'")

Why this matters: Validation doesn't mean agreement—it simply shows that you respect your partner's feelings. This helps create emotional safety, making it easier to find solutions that honor both partners' values.

4. Collaborative Solutions

Now, think of one small action each of you can take to better honor each other's priorities. The goal is to create a win-win solution that balances both needs. Even small compromises can have a big impact on reducing tension and building trust.

- **What is one small action each of you can take to better honor each other's priorities?**
    - o (Example: "Let's agree to check in on Fridays to plan our weekend together, so we can make time for both family events and career commitments.")

Why this matters: Collaborative solutions demonstrate that both partners are invested in making the relationship work. Finding creative compromises helps prevent future resentment and ensures that both people feel valued and supported.

5. Follow-Up Plan

Accountability is key to making real change. Set a plan to check in on your progress and adjust if needed. This follow-up step shows that you're both committed to honoring the changes you've agreed on and staying aligned over time.

- **When will you revisit this conversation to check on progress?**
    - o (Example: "Let's revisit this in two weeks to see how the new routine is working.")

- How will you stay accountable to the changes you've agreed on?
  - (Example: "We'll set reminders on our phones to make sure we check in every Friday.")

Why this matters: Follow-ups ensure that both partners stay engaged and committed to the changes they agreed on. This step helps create a feedback loop that keeps your relationship aligned and adaptable as new challenges arise.

Using This Exercise to Strengthen Your Relationship

Conflict is inevitable in any relationship, but it doesn't have to be a source of disconnection. By working through this worksheet, you'll gain clarity about your priorities, empathize with your partner's perspective, and find creative solutions that honor both partners. Over time, these small but meaningful changes will help you reduce tension and build a relationship rooted in mutual respect, trust, and intentional alignment.

Use this exercise regularly to reflect on conflicts as they arise and develop a habit of open communication and collaborative problem-solving. Each time you revisit it, you'll gain new insights and strengthen your connection—turning conflict into a tool for growth rather than division.

Every couple experiences conflicts over priorities, but these moments don't have to create emotional distance. In fact, they can become powerful opportunities for deeper understanding and alignment. It's natural to have differences—whether in how you manage time, money, or emotional energy—but how you approach those conflicts makes all the difference. When you shift your mindset from "winning" a disagreement to building understanding, you create space for growth and connection.

The key is to navigate conflict intentionally, using tools like curiosity, validation, and collaborative solutions. These tools allow both partners to feel seen, heard, and valued—which strengthens your bond and helps prevent resentment. You don't need to eliminate conflict entirely. Instead, the goal is to manage it constructively and use disagreements to clarify values, align priorities, and deepen trust.

The Power of Everyday Alignment

Alignment in a relationship isn't about one-time conversations or sudden breakthroughs—it's an ongoing process. Life will continue to evolve, and so will your individual priorities. What feels important today might shift as new challenges or opportunities arise. This is why regular check-ins and open communication are essential.

Creating alignment doesn't mean partners have to agree on everything—but it does mean making intentional efforts to support each other's values in everyday life. Over time, small moments of alignment—like setting boundaries around work, planning together, or validating each other's emotions—build a strong foundation of trust, connection, and mutual respect.

Looking Ahead: Tracking Effort and Building Supportive Habits

Navigating conflict zones is just the beginning. True alignment requires ongoing attention and effort. In the next chapter, we'll explore how to track effort and satisfaction across your priorities and develop supportive habits that keep your relationship aligned over time.

Nick Brancato

You'll learn how to:

- Monitor your progress to see where your efforts are working—and where you may need to adjust.
- Create habit loops that make alignment feel natural and sustainable.
- Use shared rituals and intentional practices to nurture your relationship through life's ups and downs.

Every conversation you have and every intentional action you take is a step toward deeper connection and clarity. Alignment isn't a destination—it's a journey, and each step along the way strengthens the bond you share. By staying curious, validating each other's experiences, and working collaboratively, you can build a relationship that evolves with you—one that reflects both your individual priorities and shared vision for the future.

Let's continue together and explore how to stay aligned through the natural shifts and changes that every relationship encounters.

CHAPTER 7

The Multi-Dimensional Nature of Priorities

It's not enough to rank your priorities—you also need to evaluate how satisfied you are with each one and whether you're putting in the right amount of effort to support it. Alignment isn't just about saying something is important—it's about living your values through consistent action. In this chapter, we'll explore how to assess satisfaction and effort, build habits that align with your values, and reflect on whether you and your partner feel supported in the areas that matter most.

Evaluating Satisfaction and Effort: A Roadmap to Intentional Alignment

Every priority in your life has two critical dimensions:

1. **Satisfaction** – How fulfilled or content do you feel in this area right now?
2. **Effort** – How much energy, time, and focus are you investing in this area?

Nick Brancato

It's easy to assume that more effort always leads to more satisfaction, but this isn't always the case. In reality, misalignment between satisfaction and effort is common. You might feel dissatisfied with your health but realize you're not investing enough time in exercise or self-care. On the other hand, you might pour significant effort into your career yet feel unfulfilled or burnt out because your work isn't aligned with your deeper values.

Evaluating both dimensions—satisfaction and effort—helps you identify areas where even small adjustments can lead to big improvements in your well-being and relationship. It also helps couples recognize patterns, redistribute energy more effectively, and prioritize areas that matter most.

Why This Exercise Matters for Couples

When partners evaluate satisfaction and effort together, they gain insight into how their priorities intersect and impact the relationship. One person might feel drained by career pressures, while the other feels emotionally disconnected because of a lack of quality time together. These patterns, when left unexamined, can cause tension, frustration, or resentment.

The goal of this exercise is to help you and your partner spot areas of imbalance—both as individuals and as a couple—and make intentional adjustments. You'll be able to see where energy is being wasted, where neglect may be causing dissatisfaction, and where rebalancing efforts can improve not only personal well-being but also the health of your relationship.

Satisfaction and Effort Evaluation for the 10 Core Priorities

Instructions: For each of the following priorities, rate:

- **Satisfaction (1–10):** How satisfied are you with this area of your life or relationship? (1 = Very Dissatisfied, 10 = Extremely Satisfied)
- **Effort (1–10):** How much effort are you investing in this area? (1 = Minimal Effort, 10 = Maximum Effort)

Use this tool to identify areas that may need more focus or celebrate where you're thriving. Comparing scores as a couple will help reveal alignment gaps and areas for improvement.

The 10 Core Priorities for Evaluation

Priority	Satisfaction (1–10)	Effort (1–10)
Career		
Communication		
Entertainment		
Finances		
Growth		
Health		
Relationships		
Safety		
Sex		
Spirituality		

How to Use the Evaluation

1. Identify Strengths and Areas for Adjustment

- High Satisfaction, High Effort: Celebrate your wins! This area is working well because you're investing in it intentionally.
- Low Satisfaction, High Effort: You may need to reassess your strategy. Is the effort misplaced, or do you need to shift expectations?
- High Satisfaction, Low Effort: Enjoy the ease but keep an eye on complacency—some areas may need extra attention over time.
- Low Satisfaction, Low Effort: This area might need more focus if it still matters to you. Otherwise, it's time to discuss whether it's a shared priority.

2. Compare as a Couple

- Where do your scores align? These are likely shared strengths or priorities that feel satisfying for both of you.
- Where do your scores differ? Discuss why one partner may feel more fulfilled or invested in certain areas. This insight will help you realign expectations and effort.

3. Plan Intentional Adjustments

- Choose 1-2 areas to focus on together. Create a simple plan to either increase effort where satisfaction is low or shift energy where it isn't paying off.

Example Reflections

- **Communication:** Satisfaction: 6, Effort: 8

o "We're trying to improve how we communicate, but it's still not clicking. Let's work on more specific ways to listen without interrupting."
- **Entertainment:** Satisfaction: 5, Effort: 3
  o "We're not making enough time for fun. Maybe we can schedule something light, like a weekly movie night."
- **Sex:** Satisfaction: 7, Effort: 6
  o "Things feel good, but there's room to explore new ways to connect. Let's make it a point to talk about what we both enjoy."

Spotting Patterns and Making Intentional Adjustments

This exercise helps couples identify patterns in how they manage their time, energy, and priorities. Some key questions to explore:

- Are there areas where you're both feeling drained but still unfulfilled? (Example: High effort in relationships but low satisfaction may mean you need to change how you connect.)
- Are there priorities you're neglecting that deserve more attention? (Example: Both partners may realize they need to focus more on their health.)
- Are there areas where you're over-investing energy without seeing meaningful returns? (Example: You might both be spending too much time on work and need to create stronger boundaries.)

Once you've identified these patterns, discuss how you can redistribute your energy more intentionally. For example, if both partners feel exhausted from work, you might agree to set workfree hours during the evenings. If one partner feels disconnected due to a lack of quality time, you could schedule regular date nights to reconnect.

Using the Evaluation for Growth

This exercise isn't just about identifying where things are out of balance—it's about creating intentional plans to improve alignment. By seeing the big picture of where satisfaction and effort meet or diverge, you can make more conscious choices about where to focus your energy moving forward.

Use the insights from this worksheet to make small, meaningful changes that support both individual and relationship well-being. Some examples of intentional shifts include:

- Cutting back on work hours to prioritize health and relationships.
- Rebalancing financial efforts—reducing unnecessary stress while still planning for the future.
- Adjusting your approach to communication—adding regular emotional check-ins if one partner feels unheard.

Follow-Up: Revisit the Evaluation Periodically

Alignment is an ongoing process, and priorities will continue to evolve. Revisit this evaluation regularly to track progress and make adjustments as needed. This regular reflection will help you and your partner stay in sync, ensuring that both effort and satisfaction remain aligned with your values and goals.

By using this framework regularly, you'll develop the habit of intentional living—focusing your energy on what matters most and creating a relationship that reflects both personal fulfillment and shared alignment.

Aligning Values with Habits

Once you've identified areas where your effort and satisfaction are misaligned, the next step is to align your daily habits with your values. It's easy to feel frustrated when your actions don't reflect what matters most to you. The solution lies in building intentional habits that close the gap between where you are now and where you want to be. These small, consistent habits ensure that your priorities become part of your daily life rather than distant aspirations.

Creating habits that align with your values helps both you and your partner stay connected to what matters most—both individually and as a couple. Even small actions, when done consistently, can have a profound impact over time.

Steps to Align Your Habits with Your Values

Below are five steps to help you create habits that support your priorities and bring more intentionality to your daily routine.

1. Identify a Small Habit to Reinforce Each Priority

The key to sustainable change is starting small. Choose one small, manageable habit for each priority that reflects its importance. You don't need to overhaul your life overnight—small, consistent actions will create momentum over time.

- Example:
    - If "Health" is one of your top priorities, commit to a 15-minute walk three times a week or drink a glass of water first thing in the morning.
    - If "Relationships" is a key focus, make it a habit to text a loved one once a day or plan a coffee date with a friend once a month.

Nick Brancato

Why it works: Starting with small habits makes the process feel manageable and sustainable. As these habits become routine, you'll feel more connected to your values and empowered to take on larger actions.

2. Create Rituals to Support Connection

Rituals are intentional routines that bring meaning to your day and help you stay aligned with shared priorities. For couples, rituals reinforce connection and communication, creating regular opportunities to nurture the relationship.

- **Example:**
    - If you both value Communication, create a ritual of weekly check-ins where you discuss what's going well and what areas need attention.
    - If Quality Time is important, build a habit of sitting down for dinner together without screens at least a few nights a week.

Why it works: Rituals are more than just habits—they are intentional moments of connection that remind you of your shared priorities. These routines become anchors in your relationship, helping you feel grounded and connected, even when life gets busy.

3. Reduce Habits That Conflict with Your Values

It's not just about building new habits—some current routines might be in conflict with your priorities. Identifying and reducing these habits is just as important as adding new ones. Often, these conflicting habits happen unconsciously, like mindless scrolling or overcommitting to obligations that don't align with your values.

- Example:
    o If "Relationships" is a priority, but you spend most evenings scrolling on your phone, replace that habit with screen-free time with your partner.
    o If "Health" is important, but you find yourself regularly skipping meals or eating fast food, commit to meal-prepping once a week instead.

Why it works: By identifying and reducing habits that don't align with your priorities, you free up energy for the things that matter most. These small changes can make a big difference in how satisfied you feel in your daily life.

4. Build Accountability Through Micro-Habits

Motivation alone isn't enough to sustain change over time. Micro-habits—small, easily achievable actions—help you stay consistent without relying on willpower. These micro-habits become automatic behaviors that reinforce your priorities without feeling overwhelming.

- Example:
    o If Finances is a shared priority, make it a habit to review your budget every Sunday evening.
    o If Personal Growth is important, commit to reading just one page a day from a book that inspires you.

Why it works: Micro-habits take the pressure off by focusing on small, consistent actions that are easy to maintain. Over time, these habits build momentum, helping you stay aligned without feeling overwhelmed.

5. Celebrate Progress, Not Perfection

Alignment is an ongoing process, not a one-time achievement. It's important to celebrate small wins along the way, even if you're not perfect. Recognizing progress keeps you motivated and reminds you that every step counts. Progress, not perfection, is what creates long-lasting alignment with your values.

- Example:
    o If you've committed to walking three times a week but only managed twice, acknowledge the effort and adjust for next week.
    o Celebrate small relationship wins, like successfully sticking to a weekly check-in or sharing quality time, even if other areas still need work.

Why it works: Celebrating progress shifts the focus from what's lacking to what's working. It reinforces positive behavior and helps you stay motivated and resilient when setbacks occur.

A Sustainable Path to Alignment

Aligning your habits with your values is about living intentionally. It's not about making drastic changes overnight—it's about small, meaningful actions that accumulate over time to reflect what matters most to you. As you and your partner build habits that support your shared priorities, you'll notice a deeper sense of satisfaction and connection in your relationship.

By:

- Starting small,
- Creating rituals that reinforce connection,
- Eliminating habits that don't align,
- Focusing on micro-habits, and

- Celebrating progress instead of perfection,
  you'll create a framework for living in alignment with your individual and shared values. This process brings clarity, fulfillment, and balance—not only to your personal life but to your relationship as well.

Reflection Questions: Are We Devoting the Right Amount of Effort?

It's easy to fall into routines that don't fully reflect your priorities—whether from habit, social pressure, or competing responsibilities. Taking time to pause and reflect on how you're allocating your energy allows you to see whether your actions align with your values and where adjustments are needed. These reflection questions are designed to spark meaningful conversations with yourself and your partner about where you're satisfied with the balance you've created—and where you might need to redistribute effort to feel more fulfilled.

How These Questions Strengthen Alignment

These reflection questions give you and your partner an opportunity to pause, reflect, and reconnect with your priorities. Life is constantly evolving, and it's easy to drift out of alignment without even realizing it. Regularly checking in with these questions allows you to:

- Identify areas that need more attention—whether individually or as a couple.
- Redistribute effort more intentionally, ensuring you're spending time on what truly matters.
- Support each other more effectively, even when your priorities differ.

These conversations aren't just about managing time or effort— they're about building a relationship where both partners feel valued, understood, and supported. Alignment isn't a one-time achievement; it's an ongoing process that evolves as your priorities shift and grow.

Individual Reflection Questions

Use the following prompts to check in with yourself and gain clarity on whether the way you're spending time and energy aligns with what you truly value. This exercise will help you identify misalignments between effort and satisfaction and explore opportunities for change.

1. Which priority feels most neglected right now?

- Think about the areas of life that matter most to you— whether it's health, relationships, finances, or personal growth. Which one isn't getting the attention it deserves?
- **Example:** "I've been neglecting my health because I've been prioritizing work."

2. Which area am I putting too much effort into, with little satisfaction?

- Are you overinvesting energy in an area but feeling burnt out or unfulfilled? This could point to habits that need rebalancing.
- **Example:** "I'm spending so much time on career advancement, but I feel disconnected and exhausted."

3. **Am I spending time on things that reflect my values—or things I feel obligated to do?**

   - Reflect on whether some of your actions stem from social expectations, pressure, or guilt, rather than from your authentic priorities.
   - **Example:** "I attend social events out of obligation, even though I'd rather spend that time recharging or with family."

4. **Is there one habit I could change that would bring more satisfaction?**

   - Small habit changes can lead to big improvements in how satisfied you feel. What's one thing you could shift to better align your actions with your values?
   - **Example:** "If I take 10 minutes every morning to journal or meditate, I'll feel more grounded."

Couple Reflection Questions

These prompts are designed to facilitate honest conversations between you and your partner. They'll help you evaluate the balance of your shared priorities and uncover ways to better support each other.

Use these questions to strengthen alignment and find new ways to connect meaningfully.

1. **Are we satisfied with how we're balancing our shared priorities?**

   - **Check in with each other:** Does the way you're spending time together reflect both partners' values? Or do certain shared priorities feel neglected or out of balance?

151

- **Example:** "We said relationships are a top priority, but we haven't made time for a date night in months."

2. Do we need to adjust how we spend time together to reflect what matters most?

- If life has gotten busy or routines have changed, you may need to reassess how you allocate time as a couple. Is there something you need to change or let go of to create space for what matters more?
- **Example:** "We've been spending our weekends running errands—maybe we need to carve out more time just for us."

3. How can we support each other's top priorities more effectively?

- Supporting each other doesn't always mean having the same priorities—it means finding ways to help each other feel valued. Are there small actions or gestures you could take to show support for what's important to your partner?
- **Example:** "I know your career is important to you. How can I support you more during busy work periods?"

4. Is there one small habit we could create together to strengthen our alignment?

- Small habits done together—like weekly check-ins or planning quality time—can rebuild connection and ensure both partners feel aligned. What's one small but meaningful habit you could introduce?
- **Example:** "What if we start Sunday mornings with coffee and talk about the week ahead?"

The Path to Intentional Living

By regularly engaging with these reflection questions, you and your partner create a habit of intentional alignment. These small but meaningful check-ins help you course-correct when needed, ensuring that your actions and energy reflect both your individual values and shared goals. Whether you're adjusting a small habit, creating a new routine, or simply offering support during challenging times, each conversation brings you closer to the life and relationship you truly want.

As you move forward, keep in mind that progress, not perfection, is the goal. Use these reflections as a way to stay curious and connected—to yourself, to each other, and to the priorities that matter most.

Priorities are multi-dimensional, encompassing not just what matters most but also how consistently your actions reflect those values. True alignment requires more than just identifying your priorities— it's about ensuring that your daily behaviors and decisions match your core values in ways that feel meaningful, balanced, and sustainable. This process isn't about perfection but about making intentional shifts that help you feel more connected to yourself, your partner, and the life you're building together.

By regularly evaluating both satisfaction and effort, you gain the clarity needed to rebalance your energy. Some areas may require more attention, while others may need less effort to reduce burnout or overwhelm. Building small, intentional habits based on these insights allows you to align your actions with your values— and these small shifts, when practiced over time, lead to deeper connection, fulfillment, and alignment.

Building Habits for an Evolving Future

In the next chapter, we'll dive deeper into how to navigate life's inevitable changes. As you experience shifts—whether it's a new job, becoming a parent, or entering a different stage of life—your priorities will naturally evolve. The habits and routines you build today serve as anchors that will help you stay grounded and aligned as you adjust to new realities.

You'll learn how to:

- Adapt priorities as circumstances change.
- Communicate openly about evolving needs with your partner.
- Maintain alignment by tweaking habits and routines to fit new situations.

Your Foundation for Long-Term Alignment

The work you're doing now—evaluating your priorities, rebalancing effort, and building intentional habits—is creating a strong foundation for long-term alignment. No matter what life throws your way, these tools will help you and your partner navigate changes with confidence and stay connected to your values.

Alignment isn't about getting everything right all the time—it's about staying intentional, curious, and adaptable. Each small step you take toward greater alignment strengthens your connection to your values, your partner, and your shared vision for the future. Let's continue by exploring how to navigate life's changes while maintaining the balance and clarity you've worked hard to build.

CHAPTER 8

Navigating Life Changes and Evolving Priorities

Life is full of transitions—marriage, children, career shifts, retirement, and more. Each of these milestones shapes the way we view the world and alters what we prioritize. A couple's ability to recognize and adapt to these changing priorities is essential to maintaining a healthy, balanced relationship. In this chapter, we'll explore how major life events affect priorities, why it's important to revisit the Prioritize Us Test periodically, and how couples can set goals that support their evolving needs.

The Impact of Major Life Events on Priorities

Every stage of life introduces new demands, challenges, and opportunities, causing shifts in personal and relationship priorities. What once felt essential may become less important as new responsibilities and desires emerge. These changes can create both growth opportunities and tension within relationships, especially if partners aren't intentional about reassessing priorities and adjusting habits. By understanding how life events affect priorities, couples can adapt with greater ease and stay connected, even in the midst of transformation.

Nick Brancato

Below are some key life events that commonly shift priorities, along with strategies to help couples navigate them intentionally.

1. Marriage: Building a Life Together

In the early stages of marriage, couples often focus on building emotional connection and creating shared routines. Priorities may center around romance, communication, and quality time as partners work to strengthen their bond and establish the foundation for a shared life. However, as the relationship progresses, other responsibilities—such as financial planning, buying a home, or career advancement—often take center stage.

- Challenges:
    o The need to balance practical concerns (like finances and household management) with maintaining a sense of romance and emotional intimacy.
    o As couples focus more on future planning, it's easy for communication or quality time to slip into the background.
- Strategy:
    o Intentional rituals—like regular date nights or weekend getaways—help couples maintain romance and connection, even as they focus on building a life together.
    o Financial planning together can also strengthen the relationship by reinforcing trust and shared goals.

2. Children: Adapting to Parenthood

Becoming parents is one of the most transformative life events for couples. Suddenly, priorities shift toward family, safety, and

156

financial security, with much of the couple's energy focused on raising and nurturing their children. In this phase, personal growth, entertainment, or intimacy may take a backseat, and partners may feel disconnected if they don't intentionally make time for their relationship.

- Challenges:
  - o With the demands of parenting, it can be easy for couples to feel exhausted, overwhelmed, or emotionally disconnected.
  - o Tension may arise if one partner feels that their personal needs or the relationship itself is being neglected.
- Strategy:
  - o Carve out intentional couple time, even if it's small—like 10 minutes of uninterrupted conversation each evening or a monthly date night.
  - o Communicate openly about changing needs and expectations, recognizing that priorities will shift throughout different stages of parenthood.

3. Career Changes: Balancing Work and Life

Career changes—whether it's a promotion, job loss, career shift, or starting a business—can have a major impact on personal and relationship priorities. A new role might demand more time and energy, pulling focus away from other areas such as health, relationships, or entertainment. At the same time, career changes can also offer opportunities for growth, financial stability, or personal fulfillment.

- **Challenges:**
  - o Work-life balance can become difficult to manage, leading to one partner feeling neglected or unsupported if professional demands take over.
  - o Career setbacks—like job loss—can create financial stress and affect emotional well-being, straining the relationship.
- **Strategy:**
  - o Set clear boundaries around work hours to ensure that personal time is protected.
  - o Use weekly check-ins to communicate about upcoming work commitments and discuss how both partners can support each other during busy periods or professional transitions.

4. Retirement: Redefining Roles and Routines

Retirement brings a shift in priorities, as people transition from career-driven goals to focusing on health, personal growth, or relationships. This stage offers couples more time to spend together, but it also requires adjusting routines and redefining roles—which can lead to unexpected tension if not managed intentionally.

- **Challenges:**
  - o Couples may struggle to adjust to spending more time together, especially if their routines and roles shift dramatically.
  - o One or both partners may experience identity loss or feel uncertain about how to fill their time meaningfully after retiring from long-term careers.

- Strategy:
    - Create new shared routines that foster connection, such as joining a class together, volunteering, or traveling.
    - Encourage individual pursuits that give each partner time for personal interests and growth, ensuring that both people feel fulfilled in retirement.

Adapting Priorities Through Life's Transitions

Every major life event introduces new priorities, and the ability to reassess and adjust is key to staying connected as a couple. It's important to remember that priorities are fluid—what matters most during one phase of life may evolve as circumstances change. The goal is to navigate these transitions with empathy and intention, ensuring that both partners feel supported and aligned as life evolves.

Strategies for Staying Aligned Through Change

Here are some practical tips to help couples navigate shifting priorities during life transitions:

5. Revisit Your Priorities Regularly:

- Life changes quickly—make it a habit to check in every few months about what's most important to each of you. This helps ensure that your actions reflect your evolving priorities.

6. Communicate About Expectations:

- Transitions often bring unspoken expectations. Talk openly about what you both need during these phases—whether it's more emotional support, quality time, or personal space.

7. Create Routines That Support Change:

- Whether you're adjusting to a new baby, a career shift, or retirement, build routines that reflect your new reality. For example, if you're busier at work, schedule time to reconnect on weekends.

8. Give Each Other Grace:

- Change is hard, and it's normal for one or both partners to struggle during transitions. Be patient with each other and acknowledge that adjusting priorities takes time.

9. Celebrate Milestones Together:

- Recognize and celebrate the small wins along the way—whether it's surviving the first few months of parenthood or building a new routine in retirement. Celebrating milestones helps reinforce connection and shared purpose.

Revisiting the Test Periodically: A Tool for Continuous Alignment

Your priorities will shift over time as you move through different phases of life. What feels most important today may change in six months or a year—and that's completely normal. New experiences, challenges, and opportunities often introduce new priorities or change the way you view existing ones. That's why it's essential to revisit the Prioritize Us Test periodically. Doing so allows you and your partner to check in, reconnect, and recalibrate your priorities as life evolves.

Taking the test regularly helps you stay ahead of potential misalignments, preventing small differences from becoming major sources of tension. It also creates space to celebrate areas of alignment and adjust your goals and habits to reflect your current season of life.

When Should You Take the Test Again?

There are certain key moments when it's especially helpful to reassess your priorities. Below are some life events and transitions that can significantly impact your values, habits, and relationship dynamics. Revisiting the test during these times ensures that both partners remain aligned and connected through change.

1. After a Big Life Event

Major milestones—such as marriage, the birth of a child, a job change, or retirement—can create new priorities and shift your focus. For example, starting a new job might temporarily increase your focus on career, while the birth of a child often shifts attention toward family and financial security.

Revisiting the test after these events helps ensure that both partners are on the same page about what matters most.

- **Example:** After having a baby, a couple might realize they need to shift time away from social activities to focus more on family routines and rest.

161

2. During Major Transitions

Transitions like moving to a new city, children starting school, or caring for aging parents often come with new responsibilities and emotional demands. These moments can create tension if partners don't communicate about shifting priorities and how they'll support each other through the changes. Taking the test during a transition offers clarity about what's important to each of you and helps you navigate the shift with intentionality.

- **Example:** If one partner's focus shifts toward supporting aging parents, the couple may need to adjust how they spend time together or set boundaries around work commitments.

3. Whenever Things Feel "Off" in Your Relationship

Sometimes, you can sense when something feels "off" in your relationship—whether it's recurring conflicts, growing tension, or emotional distance. Often, these challenges stem from unspoken changes in priorities or unmet expectations. Taking the test during these moments can help you pinpoint the source of friction and realign your goals and habits to restore balance and connection.

- **Example:** A couple might discover that one partner has been prioritizing personal growth more recently, while the other feels neglected because quality time has been reduced.

4. As Part of an Annual Check-In

Even if everything seems to be going smoothly, setting aside time for an annual check-in is a powerful way to maintain intentional alignment. Just as you might review your financial goals or health habits each year, reflecting on your priorities as a couple ensures that you stay connected and avoid drifting into complacency.

- **Example:** During an annual check-in, a couple might realize that entertainment and hobbies have taken a backseat and decide to start a new shared activity, like learning a language or joining a fitness class.

The Benefits of Revisiting the Test Regularly

1. Prevents Small Misalignments from Growing into Major Conflicts

- Taking the test regularly helps you catch small misalignments early before they lead to bigger issues. Recognizing these areas early allows you to make adjustments before resentment builds.

2. Promotes Continuous Growth and Adaptation

- Life will continue to change, and so will your priorities. Revisiting the test ensures that your relationship evolves along with you, fostering flexibility and growth over time.

3. Strengthens Communication and Connection

- Each time you take the test, you have an opportunity to connect through meaningful conversations about what's working, what's changed, and what still needs attention. These discussions strengthen emotional intimacy and mutual understanding.

4. Reinforces a Sense of Shared Purpose

- Regularly checking in on your priorities reminds both partners of the bigger picture—the shared vision and goals that brought you together. This helps you feel more aligned, even during challenging seasons.

How to Approach the Test Check-Ins

To get the most out of your periodic check-ins, approach the conversation with openness and curiosity. Here are some tips for making these moments productive and meaningful:

- **Create a Relaxed Environment:** Choose a quiet time when you both feel calm and open to conversation—perhaps during a weekend morning with coffee or during a walk together.
- **Acknowledge Change as Normal:** It's important to remind each other that changing priorities are a natural part of growth. Approach the conversation with curiosity rather than judgment.
- **Focus on Solutions, Not Problems:** If you uncover misalignments, work together to find small, actionable ways to rebalance your efforts. Focus on what you can do moving forward rather than dwelling on past frustrations.

Examples of Changing Priorities: Couples Who Adapted and Thrived

When life shifts, priorities shift too. Couples who adapt and thrive are those who remain open to change, communicate intentionally, and find ways to blend their values and goals. Even when partners initially seem to be on different pages, intentional adjustments can create new paths toward connection and alignment. Let's explore two examples of couples who successfully navigated changing priorities and emerged stronger.

1. Jenna and Mark – The New Parents

When Jenna and Mark first got married, they prioritized growth, relationships, and entertainment. They spent their weekends exploring new places, trying new restaurants, and enjoying a vibrant social life with friends. But when their first child was born, everything changed. Suddenly, their priorities shifted toward health, safety, and financial security.

- Mark felt the pressure of providing for his growing family and began focusing on career and savings. He wanted to ensure their baby had everything they needed, from health care to a stable home.
- Jenna, on the other hand, struggled with feeling disconnected from her old identity. She loved her new role as a mother, but she missed the freedom and excitement of her pre-parenting life.

As the months went on, they began to feel tension. Jenna wanted to keep some of the entertainment alive, while Mark was completely focused on work obligations. They realized that unless they found a way to balance their new realities, they risked growing distant.

- **What They Did:**
    - Six months after their baby was born, Jenna and Mark decided to revisit the Prioritize Us Test.
    - The results revealed that Mark's top priorities had shifted almost entirely to financial security and career, while Jenna still placed high value on growth and entertainment.

- **How They Aligned:**
  - o Armed with these insights, they agreed to make space for both priorities. Mark committed to saving time for occasional date nights, knowing it would help them reconnect as a couple.
  - o Jenna found ways to incorporate entertainment into family life by planning weekend hikes, movies, and short trips they could enjoy together with their child.

The Outcome: These small but intentional shifts allowed both partners to feel seen and supported. Mark's focus on family and finances remained intact, but Jenna was able to keep a piece of her adventurous spirit alive. They learned that parenthood didn't have to mean giving up joy and connection—it just required adjusting how they expressed it.

2. Carlos and Diane – The Retirees

Carlos and Diane had been looking forward to retirement for years, imagining all the freedom they would have once they no longer had work responsibilities. However, once they both officially retired, they found themselves in conflict.

- Carlos envisioned retirement as a time to relax—he dreamed of slow mornings, quiet afternoons, and plenty of time to unwind. After decades of work, all he wanted was peace and comfort.
- Diane, however, had a very different vision for retirement. She wanted to travel, volunteer, and focus on self development. For her, this was a chance to stay active and explore new opportunities now that they had more time together.

Their differing expectations caused tension and disappointment in the early months. Diane felt restless and frustrated that Carlos wasn't as excited about travel and activities as she was, while Carlos felt pressured to give up the relaxation he had worked so hard for.

- **What They Did:**
    - o To get back on the same page, Carlos and Diane decided to take the Prioritize Us Test. Their results revealed that Carlos placed high value on health and safety, while Diane's priorities leaned heavily toward entertainment, and personal growth. This exercise helped them realize that neither partner's vision was wrong—they just needed to blend their priorities more intentionally.
- **How They Aligned:**
    - o Together, they created a weekly schedule that included both rest and adventure. Diane agreed to set aside time for Carlos's relaxation, ensuring he had space to unwind without guilt.
    - o In return, Carlos committed to joining Diane on a few volunteer projects and taking short trips she had been excited about.

The Outcome: By balancing both rest and activity, Carlos and Diane found a way to enjoy their retirement together. Carlos didn't have to sacrifice his downtime, and Diane felt supported in her desire to stay active and engaged. These small compromises allowed them to align their expectations and build a new routine that honored both of their needs.

Lessons from These Stories: How Couples Adapt and Thrive

The stories of Jenna and Mark, and Carlos and Diane, illustrate that changing priorities don't have to create conflict. Life will bring unexpected shifts, but with open communication and flexibility, couples can adapt and find new ways to connect. Here are a few key takeaways:

1. Priorities Will Shift—And That's Okay:

- Life events, like having children or entering retirement, naturally shift what feels most important. The key is to embrace these changes with curiosity rather than resistance.

2. Regular Check-Ins Help Prevent Misalignment:

- Both couples found success by using the Prioritize Us Test to gain clarity about each other's values and make intentional adjustments.

3. Small Changes Make a Big Difference:

- Neither couple made drastic changes—instead, they made small but meaningful shifts to align their priorities. This approach makes it easier to stay on track without feeling overwhelmed.

4. Compromise Doesn't Mean Sacrifice:

- Successful alignment isn't about one partner giving up what matters to them. It's about finding ways to blend priorities so that both people feel seen, valued, and supported.

Goal-Setting Exercise: Adapting to Future Life Changes

This exercise will help you and your partner set goals that reflect both your current priorities and the changes you anticipate in the future. Use the space below to outline specific actions you can take to stay aligned through life's transitions.

Step 1: Identify Upcoming Life Changes

Think about any changes or events that are likely to affect your priorities in the near future. Write them down here:

- _____
- _____
- _____

Step 2: List Your Current Top Priorities

Each partner should list their top three current priorities:

- Partner 1:

1. _____
2. _____
3. _____

- Partner 2:

1. _____

2. _____

3. _____

Step 3: Identify Potential Conflicts

Are there any priorities that might come into conflict as these life changes occur? Write them down below:

- _____
- _____
- _____

Step 4: Create Actionable Goals

For each potential conflict, brainstorm one or two specific actions you can take to align your priorities.

- **Example:** If a job change creates time management challenges, set a goal to schedule weekly check-ins to stay connected.
- _____
- _____

Step 5: Plan for Check-Ins

Decide when you'll revisit the Prioritize Us Test and your goals.

- Next Check-In Date: _____

From Priorities to Action: Creating a Roadmap for Alignment

Understanding your priorities is just the first step. True alignment happens when you turn those priorities into action. It's not enough to recognize what matters most—you need to translate those insights into tangible goals, routines, and habits that reflect your values in everyday life. This intentional approach helps you stay grounded in your shared vision while allowing room for individual growth.

Example of Intentional Actions:

- If "Communication" is a top priority, you could set up a weekly check-in where you discuss what's working and what needs attention in your relationship.
- If "Health" is important to both of you, you could plan active dates, like hiking or biking, to stay connected while supporting each other's well-being.

These small, intentional actions create alignment not just in theory but in practice, ensuring that your daily habits reflect your priorities.

The Power of Regular Reflection and Goal-Setting

By setting actionable goals and revisiting them regularly, you build a framework for continuous alignment. This doesn't mean your relationship will always be free from tension—life will still throw challenges your way. However, the habits you cultivate now will serve as anchors during times of change, keeping you and your partner connected even when life feels chaotic.

Looking Ahead: Turning Priorities into Tangible Action Plans

In the next chapter, we'll dive deeper into how to translate your priorities into concrete goals and action plans. With the insights you've gained so far, you're ready to take the next step toward intentional alignment. You'll learn how to:

- Set meaningful, achievable goals that reflect your values.
- Break goals into actionable steps to build momentum.
- Create supportive habits that help you stay aligned over time.
- Monitor progress and adjust as needed to stay on track.

With these tools, you'll be equipped to bring your priorities to life—building a relationship that evolves with you, supports both partners' growth, and reflects what matters most in every season.

Together, let's continue toward a more connected, intentional, and aligned relationship.

CHAPTER 9

Setting Goals and Taking Action

Knowing your priorities is just the beginning—the real power lies in turning those priorities into actionable goals and working together to achieve them. In this chapter, we'll guide you through the process of setting meaningful goals based on your priority rankings, creating a shared action plan, and tracking progress to stay accountable.

Alignment isn't just about having great conversations; it's about taking small, consistent actions that reflect what matters most to both of you.

Turning Priorities into Goals

Once you've ranked your priorities and reviewed your Total Difference Score (TDS), the next step is to turn those insights into actionable goals. It's one thing to say that "Health" or "Relationships" are important—it's another to follow through with consistent actions that reflect those priorities. Setting clear, meaningful goals helps you bridge the gap between what matters most to you and the habits and behaviors that bring those values to life.

Well-defined goals provide direction, accountability, and motivation, ensuring that both partners stay aligned as they work toward shared and individual priorities. Below, we explore three key principles for setting effective goals that reflect your values and help you stay on track.

1. Make Your Goals Specific and Actionable

Vague goals like "Spend more time together" sound good, but they're often too broad to inspire consistent action. To increase the likelihood of success, your goals should be specific and actionable —focused on a clear behavior or task you can execute. This way, both partners know exactly what needs to be done and when.

- **Vague Goal:** "We should communicate more."
- **Specific and Actionable Goal:** "We'll have a 20-minute check-in every Sunday evening to talk about the upcoming week."

Why It Works: Specific goals eliminate ambiguity, making it easier to stay on track. When you define exactly what, when, and how you'll take action, it becomes easier to integrate that behavior into your routine.

- **Example:**
    o If Health is a top priority, instead of saying, "We'll get in better shape," try: "We'll go for a 30minute walk together three mornings a week."

o   If Relationships are a focus, replace "Spend more time together" with "We'll schedule a date night every Friday without screens or distractions."

This clarity helps both partners stay committed and reduces the chance of misunderstandings about expectations.

2. Ensure Your Goals Are Measurable

Measurable goals provide a clear way to track progress and stay motivated. When you can see tangible progress, it reinforces your commitment and gives you a sense of accomplishment. Without a measurable component, it's easy to lose sight of whether you're moving forward or staying stuck.

- **Vague Goal:** "We need to save more money."
- **Measurable Goal:** "We'll save $500 each month toward our vacation fund."

Why It Works: When goals are measurable, you can celebrate small wins along the way and adjust if needed. Knowing exactly how much effort you've put in and seeing the results helps sustain motivation over time.

- **Example:**
    o   If Communication is a priority, instead of saying, "Let's talk more," try: "We'll set aside 10 minutes every evening to check in about our day."
    o   If Finances are a shared focus, commit to saving a specific amount each month or tracking your spending every week.

Tracking progress also makes it easier to course-correct if something isn't working, helping both partners stay accountable.

175

3. Set Short-Term and Long-Term Goals

Some priorities require immediate action, while others will take time to achieve. By creating a mix of short-term and long-term goals, you keep momentum high and ensure that both partners feel like progress is being made.

- **Short-Term Goals:** Focus on small, achievable actions that build confidence and create quick wins.
    - o **Example:** "Plan a weekend trip within the next two weeks."
    - o **Long-Term Goals:** These require consistent effort over time and provide direction for the future.
    - o **Example:** "Improve communication over the next six months by scheduling regular check-ins and practicing active listening."

Why It Works: Short-term goals create immediate motivation by offering small victories, while longterm goals keep you focused on bigger priorities. Working toward both types of goals simultaneously helps maintain balance—you get the satisfaction of completing smaller tasks while still moving toward longer-term objectives.

- **Example:**
    - o If Career is a priority, a short-term goal might be: "Update my resume by the end of the month." A long-term goal could be: "Secure a promotion within the next year."
    - o If Health is a priority, a short-term goal might be: "Drink more water this week." A long-term goal could be: "Run a 5K within six months."

Short-term wins build momentum, and long-term goals ensure lasting alignment with your values.

Practical Example: Turning Priorities into Goals and Actions

Let's say you and your partner have identified "Health" and "Relationships" as top priorities. Here's how you can break those priorities into specific, measurable, and time-bound goals:

- Health:
    - **Short-Term Goal:** "We'll sign up for a yoga class this week."
    - **Long-Term Goal:** "We'll participate in a local charity 5K event in six months."
- Relationships:
    - **Short-Term Goal:** "We'll plan a movie night this Saturday with no phones or distractions."
    - **Long-Term Goal:** "We'll take a weekend getaway once every three months to reconnect."

These goals offer clear direction and balance quick wins with sustained progress, helping you stay aligned with your priorities over time.

Building Habits to Support Your Goals

Once you've set your goals, the next step is to integrate them into your daily or weekly routines. Building consistent habits ensures that your goals become part of your lifestyle, rather than isolated tasks you only think about occasionally.

Nick Brancato

- **Example Habit:**
  - ○ If Finances are a shared priority, make it a habit to review your budget every Sunday evening.
  - ○ If Communication is a focus, build the habit of having a quick, daily check-in before bed.

These small habits build momentum and ensure that you're consistently working toward your goals.

Adjusting Goals as Life Changes

Your goals should be flexible enough to adapt to changing circumstances. Life events—like the birth of a child, a new job, or moving to a new city—may require adjustments to your priorities and goals. Revisit your goals regularly to ensure they still reflect what matters most to you and your partner.

- **Example:** If your original goal was to exercise five days a week, but a new job leaves you with less free time, adjust to three days a week without guilt.

The key is to stay flexible and committed to making progress, even when life throws curveballs.

Aligning Priorities with Actionable Goals

Turning priorities into tangible goals ensures that your daily efforts reflect what matters most. By setting specific, measurable, short-term, and long-term goals, you give your priorities the attention they deserve. Clear goals also help you track progress, stay motivated, and make adjustments as needed.

Goal-Setting Framework: SMART Goals

The SMART goal framework helps ensure that the goals you set are clear, actionable, and achievable. Vague intentions can be difficult to follow through on, but SMART goals provide a structured approach that makes it easier to stay focused, track progress, and achieve meaningful results. SMART goals are especially effective for couples working toward shared priorities, as they set clear expectations and create accountability for both partners.

What Are SMART Goals?

Each SMART goal contains five essential elements:

1. Specific:

- A goal should be clear and well-defined, leaving no room for ambiguity.
- Ask: What exactly do we want to accomplish?

2. Measurable:

- You should be able to track your progress toward the goal and know when you've achieved it.
- Ask: How will we measure success?

3. Achievable:

- The goal should be realistic given your current resources, time, and circumstances.
- Ask: Is this goal manageable with our current commitments?

4. Relevant:

- The goal needs to be aligned with your values and priorities to ensure it feels meaningful.
- Ask: Does this goal reflect what matters most to us right now?

5. Time-bound:

- Every goal should have a deadline or timeframe to create focus and urgency.
- Ask: When do we want to accomplish this goal?

Examples of SMART Goals by Priority Area

Here are examples of how SMART goals can be applied to different priorities, showing how to break broad intentions into specific, actionable steps.

1. Health Priority: A Fitness Goal

- SMART Goal: "We will exercise together for 30 minutes, three times a week, for the next 90 days."
- Why it Works:
  - Specific: It clearly defines the type of exercise (together for 30 minutes).
  - Measurable: Success can be tracked by counting the number of workouts per week.
  - Achievable: The goal is realistic given the time commitment.
  - Relevant: It aligns with the couple's health and fitness priorities.
  - Time-bound: The goal has a 90-day timeframe to monitor progress.

180

2. Financial Priority: Paying Down Debt

- **SMART Goal:** "We will pay off $5,000 in credit card debt by the end of the year by reducing discretionary spending and making biweekly payments."
- **Why it Works:**
    - **Specific:** The exact amount to pay off is defined ($5,000).
    - **Measurable:** Progress is measurable by tracking payments toward the debt.
    - **Achievable:** The goal is realistic if the couple adjusts spending and makes payments consistently.
    - **Relevant:** It reflects the couple's shared financial priorities and values.
    - **Time-bound:** There is a clear deadline (by the end of the year).

3. Relationships Priority: Strengthening Communication

- **SMART Goal:** "We will have a 20-minute relationship check-in every Sunday evening for the next three months to discuss our goals and address any challenges."
- **Why it Works:**
    - **Specific:** The goal defines a specific action (relationship check-in) and sets a time for it (Sunday evening).
    - **Measurable:** Success can be tracked weekly by following through with the check-ins.
    - **Achievable:** It's realistic because it only requires a 20-minute commitment each week.

- o **Relevant:** The goal aligns with the couple's focus on improving communication.
- o **Time-bound:** The goal has a timeframe of three months to evaluate its effectiveness.

4. Career Priority: Pursuing Professional Development

- SMART Goal: "I will complete an online certification course in project management within six months to enhance my career prospects."
- Why it Works:
  - o **Specific:** The goal outlines a concrete step (complete a certification course).
  - o **Measurable:** Progress can be measured by tracking course modules completed.
  - o **Achievable:** Six months provides enough time to complete the course without overwhelming other responsibilities.
  - o **Relevant:** The goal aligns with professional development priorities.
  - o **Time-bound:** It includes a six-month deadline.

Tips for Setting SMART Goals Together

1. Discuss Priorities Before Setting Goals:

- Make sure both partners are clear about their shared and individual priorities before creating goals. This will ensure alignment and prevent misunderstandings.

2. Start with Small, Manageable Goals:

- Setting smaller goals first builds momentum and gives both partners a sense of accomplishment. Once you achieve smaller goals, you can work toward larger, long-term objectives.

3. Use a Shared Calendar or App:

- To stay on track, schedule time for activities like exercise or check-ins on a shared calendar.
- This creates accountability and ensures that goals don't get lost in the busyness of daily life.

4. Celebrate Progress Along the Way:

- Acknowledge your wins, even if they're small. Celebrating progress builds motivation and keeps both partners engaged in the process.

5. Revisit and Adjust Goals Regularly:

- Life will change, and your goals may need to change too. Set time aside to check in on your progress and adjust your goals if necessary to keep them aligned with your evolving priorities.

Using SMART Goals to Strengthen Alignment

The SMART goal framework provides a practical way to translate your priorities into meaningful actions. Whether you're working on health, finances, relationships, or career goals, SMART goals help you and your partner stay focused, motivated, and aligned. By setting specific, measurable, and time-bound goals, you'll know exactly what needs to be done and how to track your progress.

The process of setting SMART goals also promotes better communication—it gives you an opportunity to discuss your expectations openly and ensure that you're on the same page. Over time, these small but intentional efforts will help you strengthen your connection and create a life that reflects your shared values.

Tracking Progress and Staying Accountable

Setting goals is only the first step—the real challenge lies in tracking progress and staying accountable over time. Life gets busy, and it's easy for good intentions to get lost in the demands of everyday routines. The key to success is monitoring your progress regularly, adjusting when needed, and staying consistent, even when setbacks occur. Accountability isn't just about staying on track; it's about creating space for open communication, mutual support, and celebrating progress along the way.

Below are five strategies to help you and your partner stay focused, motivated, and accountable as you work toward your shared and individual goals.

1. Use a Goal Tracker or Journal

Having a visual way to track your progress makes your goals feel more tangible and motivating. A shared journal, spreadsheet, or goal-tracking app allows both partners to see the progress they're making, celebrate small wins, and identify areas that need attention. Writing things down also reinforces commitment and keeps your priorities top of mind.

- Example Tools:
    o Use a habit-tracking app to log progress daily or weekly.
    o Keep a shared journal to record milestones, challenges, and reflections on what's working and what isn't.

Why It Works: Tracking progress in real time helps you stay connected to your goals and builds a sense of momentum. Even seeing small improvements—like sticking to your savings plan or hitting a fitness milestone—can boost motivation and encourage you to keep going.

2. Schedule Regular Check-Ins

Regular check-ins keep you and your partner accountable by providing structured time to reflect on progress, discuss challenges, and adjust goals if needed. Whether it's a weekly, biweekly, or monthly check-in, these conversations help you stay aligned and ensure that both partners feel supported in their efforts.

- Example:
    o "How are we doing with our fitness goals? Should we adjust our schedule to make time for more morning workouts?"
    o "Are we still on track with our savings goal, or do we need to tweak our budget?"

Tips for Effective Check-Ins:

- Keep it positive and solution-focused—focus on what's working and how you can overcome challenges.

- Use your check-ins to realign priorities if circumstances have changed.
- Set reminders on your phone or calendar to ensure that check-ins happen consistently.

Why It Works: Scheduling regular check-ins keeps communication open and proactive, preventing small issues from growing into major frustrations. It also reinforces the idea that goal-setting is a shared experience, not an individual task.

3. Acknowledge Setbacks Without Blame

Life is unpredictable, and you won't hit every goal on the first try—and that's okay. Setbacks are a normal part of the process. What matters is how you respond to them. Instead of assigning blame, treat setbacks as opportunities for learning and problem-solving. Discuss what didn't work, explore ways to adjust your approach, and move forward with a renewed plan.

- **Example Conversation:**
  - o "We missed two workout sessions last week—what got in the way? Should we try exercising earlier in the day next time?"
  - o "We overspent on entertainment this month. Let's brainstorm ways to cut back next month without feeling restricted."

Why It Works: When you remove blame from the conversation, it's easier to stay positive and collaborative. A problem-solving approach fosters trust and helps both partners feel safe and supported, even when things don't go perfectly.

4. Adjust Goals as Priorities Evolve

Your goals should reflect your current values and circumstances—but life is always changing. As new opportunities, challenges, or transitions arise, some goals may need to be adjusted or replaced. Regularly revisiting your goals ensures that they remain relevant and achievable. If a particular goal no longer aligns with your priorities, it's okay to let it go or shift your focus to something else.

- Example:
    - "Now that we've welcomed our new baby, let's shift our goal from traveling abroad to planning local family adventures."
    - "Since you're starting a new job, let's adjust our fitness goal to three workouts a week instead of five until you get settled."

Why It Works: Flexibility is key to maintaining momentum. Goals that worked six months ago may not fit your current reality, and adapting them allows you to stay aligned without feeling discouraged. Revisiting your goals regularly ensures that they continue to reflect your priorities as they evolve.

5. Celebrate Milestones Together

Don't wait until you've completed the entire goal to celebrate—acknowledge progress along the way. Small wins, like sticking to a new habit for a week or saving your first $1,000, deserve recognition. Celebrating these moments boosts motivation and reinforces the positive behaviors you want to maintain.

- Ideas for Celebrating Milestones:
    - Treat yourselves to a nice dinner after completing your first month of workouts.

187

- o Celebrate financial progress by planning a budget-friendly date night.
- o Take a weekend getaway to mark progress toward long-term goals, like paying off a chunk of debt or reaching a savings milestone.

Why It Works: Celebrating progress builds momentum and strengthens your bond as a couple. It reminds both partners that the path toward your goals is just as important as the destination, reinforcing a sense of shared purpose and joy in working together.

Accountability as a Foundation for Success

Tracking progress and staying accountable transforms good intentions into meaningful action. It ensures that your goals don't get lost in the shuffle of daily life and keeps you focused on what matters most. By using tools like goal trackers, regular check-ins, and celebrating milestones, you create a framework that helps both partners stay motivated and connected.

Accountability isn't about perfection—it's about staying committed to your priorities and being flexible enough to adjust when life changes. When you approach setbacks with curiosity, realign your goals as needed, and celebrate progress along the way, you create a sustainable path toward growth and alignment.

Example: Tracking Progress in Real Life – Ben and Mia

Let's revisit Ben and Mia's story. After taking the Prioritize Us Test, they identified health and financial security as top priorities but realized that their actions weren't aligning with these values. They had been neglecting workouts and didn't have a solid savings plan in place. Together, they decided to create specific, shared

188

goals to help them stay accountable and better reflect their priorities.

Ben and Mia's Shared Goals

1. Health Goal:

- "We will work out together three times a week for 30 minutes."

2. Finance Goal:

- "We will save $5,000 for an emergency fund within 10 months."

How They Tracked Progress and Stayed Accountable

Ben and Mia knew that simply setting goals wasn't enough—they needed a way to track their progress, stay motivated, and make adjustments along the way. Below is how they approached the process in a way that ensured both accountability and connection.

1. Weekly Check-Ins to Stay on Track

Every Sunday evening, Ben and Mia made it a habit to review their workout schedule and budget together. This gave them a chance to reflect on their progress, troubleshoot any challenges, and celebrate small wins.

- Example Conversation:
    - o **Ben:** "We only worked out once this week—what got in the way?"

      ○ **Mia:** "I think we overcommitted with evening plans. Maybe we should try morning workouts instead?"

They used these check-ins to brainstorm solutions rather than assigning blame, ensuring that setbacks became opportunities for problem-solving rather than sources of frustration.

Why It Worked: The weekly check-ins gave Ben and Mia a structured way to stay connected to their goals without feeling overwhelmed. This regular touchpoint helped them catch misalignments early and adjust their plans before small issues became major roadblocks.

2. Making Adjustments to Fit Their Busy Schedule

After six weeks, Ben and Mia realized that 30-minute workouts were becoming difficult to fit into their schedule, especially on busy days. Rather than giving up, they adjusted their plan:

- **New Plan:** They switched to 20-minute home workouts that were more flexible and easier to complete.

This small change helped them stay consistent without sacrificing progress, showing that flexibility is key to long-term success.

Why It Worked: Adjusting their workouts made the goal more achievable, helping them stay motivated rather than feeling discouraged. This also reinforced the idea that perfection isn't necessary—it's more important to stay engaged and adaptable.

3. Celebrating Progress with Small Rewards

Ben and Mia didn't wait until they reached their final goal to celebrate—they knew that acknowledging small wins along the way would help them stay motivated and connected.

- **First Milestone:** After saving their first $1,000, they celebrated with a picnic in the park, a lowcost reward that allowed them to reflect on their progress together.

During the picnic, they talked about how good it felt to see their savings grow and how much more in control they felt over their finances.

Why It Worked: Celebrating progress gave them a sense of accomplishment and reinforced their commitment to their shared goals. It also created an opportunity for emotional connection—reminding them that working toward their priorities could also be fun and rewarding.

The Outcome: Staying on Track and Strengthening Their Connection

By tracking their progress, adjusting their plans when needed, and celebrating small wins, Ben and Mia were able to stay on track with their health and financial goals. But more importantly, the process strengthened their relationship.

- **Improved Communication:** The weekly check-ins became a natural space for open conversations about their goals, challenges, and progress.
- **Mutual Support:** Each partner felt supported rather than criticized, which deepened their trust and connection.

- **Shared Accomplishment:** Working together toward common goals gave them a sense of shared purpose, reinforcing their bond as a team.

By staying flexible and committed, Ben and Mia learned that goal-setting isn't just about achieving outcomes—it's about creating alignment, building trust, and enjoying the process together.

Key Takeaways from Ben and Mia's Story

1. Consistency Over Perfection:

- It's okay to adjust goals as life changes. What matters most is staying engaged and consistent.

2. Check-Ins Build Connection:

- Regular conversations about progress help partners stay on the same page and create opportunities to problem-solve together.

3. Celebrate Small Wins:

- Acknowledging milestones—even small ones—builds motivation and makes life more enjoyable.

4. Flexibility is Key:

- Adjusting plans when needed ensures that life's challenges don't derail your progress.

Tracking Progress for Long-Term Success

Ben and Mia's story shows that tracking progress, staying accountable, and celebrating milestones can make a significant difference—not just in achieving goals, but in deepening your connection as a couple. Goals are not just about outcomes—they are a tool for growth, communication, and alignment.

Whether you're working toward health, financial, or relationship goals, the key is to stay flexible, check in regularly, and celebrate your progress. With these strategies in place, you and your partner will be better equipped to navigate challenges, stay aligned, and enjoy the process of working toward your shared vision.

Setting goals that align with your priorities is the bridge between good intentions and meaningful action. It's not just about knowing what matters most—it's about doing the work together to bring those priorities to life. A shared action plan creates clarity and ensures that both partners stay engaged, accountable, and connected as they pursue their individual and relationship goals.

The process doesn't end with setting goals; tracking progress and making adjustments along the way is essential to keep things on track. Life will inevitably get busy, and unexpected challenges will arise, but with intentional tracking, regular check-ins, and flexibility, you and your partner can stay aligned and make steady progress, even during life's busiest seasons.

Alignment is not a one-time destination—it's an ongoing process of reflecting, adjusting, and growing together. Priorities will shift, circumstances will change, and new challenges will emerge, but what matters is that both partners remain committed to navigating these changes with empathy and intention.

Celebrating Alignment and Growth

In a relationship, alignment and growth are ongoing processes— and every intentional step you take together is worth recognizing. Celebrating your progress reinforces the importance of living by your shared values and strengthens the bond between you and your partner. Whether it's a small win or a major milestone, acknowledging these moments builds momentum and motivation to stay on track. Celebrations also remind both partners that the path toward alignment is not just about reaching goals —it's about finding joy and connection along the way.

Below are meaningful ways to celebrate your alignment and growth as a couple.

1. Acknowledge Small Wins

Small wins are the building blocks of long-term success. Each time you follow through on a goal or make an intentional choice that reflects your priorities, it's a step in the right direction. Recognizing these moments, no matter how small, reinforces positive habits and reminds you of the progress you're making together.

- How to Acknowledge Small Wins:
    - Take a moment to express gratitude when you notice your partner staying consistent with a goal or priority.
    - Offer encouragement by recognizing how far you've come—whether it's sticking to weekly check-ins or saving a little extra money.
- Example:
    - "I noticed we've been really consistent with our Sunday check-ins, and it's made me feel so much more connected to you."
    - "I'm proud of us for sticking to our workout routine. Even on busy weeks, we're finding ways to stay active together."

Why It Works: Acknowledging small wins boosts morale and reinforces that you're on the right path. It also helps you both feel appreciated and supported, making it easier to stay committed to your shared goals.

2. Celebrate Milestones with Meaningful Experiences

Major milestones—like reducing your TDS score, reaching a financial goal, or navigating a life transition —deserve more than just a quick acknowledgment. Celebrate these moments with experiences that reflect your values, creating meaningful memories that reinforce your connection and the progress you've made.

- How to Celebrate Milestones:
    - Think about what experiences align with your shared priorities. If you both value adventure, plan a weekend getaway. If relationships are a focus, host a small celebration with loved ones.
    - Choose experiences that strengthen your bond— whether it's something new you do together or a ritual you enjoy regularly.
- Example:
    - If adventure is a shared value: Plan a weekend hiking trip or explore a new city together.
    - If relationships are important: Host a gathering with family and friends to celebrate a shared achievement, like paying off debt or moving to a new home.

Why It Works: Celebrating milestones through meaningful experiences creates lasting memories and reinforces the idea that alignment isn't just about goals—it's about living intentionally and enjoying life together.

3. Reflect on Moments of Growth

Looking back on your past helps you appreciate the progress you've made—especially during challenging times. Reflecting on growth allows you to recognize how you've overcome obstacles, adapted to changes, and become stronger as a couple. These moments of reflection build confidence for the future and show you that, together, you can navigate whatever comes your way.

- **How to Reflect on Growth:**
    - o Schedule time to sit down and reflect on your past as a couple. What challenges have you overcome? What goals have you achieved?
    - o Talk about how your priorities have evolved over time and what you've learned from the process.
- **Example:**
    - o "A year ago, we were really struggling to balance work and quality time. But now we've found a rhythm that works for both of us, and I feel so much closer to you."
    - o "I love how we've made saving money feel like a team effort. We've come a long way, and it's exciting to see how our hard work is paying off."

Why It Works: Reflecting on moments of growth helps you see your journey as a couple in perspective. It builds confidence, strengthens trust, and motivates you to keep growing together, knowing that you've already overcome challenges in the past.

Additional Ideas for Celebrating Alignment and Growth

- Create a Visual Reminder:
  - o Make a vision board or progress tracker that highlights your shared priorities and achievements. Hang it somewhere visible to keep both partners inspired.
  - o Example: Use a savings tracker to mark milestones as you reach financial goals.
- Start a Celebration Ritual:
  - o Create a celebration ritual for milestones—like ordering takeout from your favorite restaurant or writing each other appreciation notes on small wins.
  - o Example: At the end of each month, reflect together over coffee or dessert on what you accomplished that month.
- Share Your Wins with Others:
  - o Sometimes, sharing your achievements with friends or family can make the moment even more special. Letting loved ones know about your progress reinforces the importance of your goals and strengthens your support network.

The Power of Celebration: Building Joy and Connection

Celebrating alignment and growth isn't just about rewarding achievements—it's about enjoying the process and deepening your connection. When you acknowledge small wins, reflect on growth, and celebrate meaningful milestones, you create positive reinforcement that motivates both partners to stay aligned with their values.

These celebrations also remind you that the journey matters as much as the destination. Working toward alignment isn't just about achieving perfect outcomes—it's about growing together, learning from each other, and making intentional choices that reflect who you are as individuals and as a couple.

The Power of Ongoing Reflection

Here are practical ways to integrate ongoing reflection into your relationship and ensure you stay aligned, no matter what life brings.

1. Schedule Monthly or Annual Check-Ins

Just as companies conduct regular evaluations to ensure they're on track with goals, couples benefit from periodic check-ins to revisit their shared priorities. These moments allow you to reflect on your individual and collective growth, identify areas that need attention, and make intentional adjustments before conflicts arise.

- **How to Do It:**
    - Set aside time every month or once a year to take the Prioritize Us Test again.
    - Use the results to explore how your priorities have shifted and adjust your goals and routines accordingly.
- **Example Conversations:**
    - "Now that we've moved to a new city, let's revisit our priorities to see what we need to focus on."
    - "Since we're thinking about starting a family, maybe we need to adjust our financial goals."

Why It Works: Regular check-ins help you catch misalignments early and make adjustments proactively rather than waiting for tensions to build. These moments also create space for celebrating progress and strengthening your bond.

2. Create a Reflection Ritual

Reflection becomes easier when it's woven into your routine. Establishing a regular reflection ritual ensures that you and your partner stay connected to your priorities and course-correct when necessary. These rituals don't have to be complicated—they just need to provide space for intentional conversations.

- Ideas for Reflection Rituals:
    - o Weekly check-ins over coffee to discuss what's working and what's not.
    - o Sunday evening reflections where you review goals and set intentions for the week ahead.
    - o Monthly goal reviews to track progress and adjust any habits or priorities that need fine-tuning.
- Example Conversation:
    - o "How are we feeling about our schedule this week? Do we need to shift anything to make more time for each other?"

Why It Works: A regular ritual ensures that reflection becomes a habit, not an afterthought. These moments also foster ongoing communication and reduce the chance of small issues turning into larger conflicts.

3. Notice Patterns and Course-Correct Early

Recurring conflicts often signal deeper misalignments. When you notice the same disagreements or frustrations cropping up repeatedly, it's likely that one or both partners' priorities have shifted without being fully acknowledged. Pay attention to these patterns and use them as opportunities to coursecorrect before resentment builds.

- **How to Use Reflection During Conflict:**
  - When a recurring conflict arises, pause and ask:
  - "Is there a shift in one of our priorities that we haven't addressed yet?" ▪ "What new need or value is showing up that we need to talk about?"
- **Example:**
  - If you've been arguing about how much time you're spending on work vs. family, it might indicate that family time is becoming a higher priority for one of you—and the routine needs to reflect that shift.

Why It Works: By addressing misalignments early, you can avoid unnecessary tension and adapt your goals before they become sources of frustration. Recognizing these patterns helps you stay proactive, not reactive, and strengthens your ability to navigate change together.

Growing Together Through Reflection

The journey toward alignment isn't about achieving a perfect balance once and for all—it's about staying engaged with each other through ongoing reflection. Life will continue to shift, bringing new challenges and opportunities, but regular check-ins ensure that both partners can adapt together with intention and clarity. By scheduling periodic evaluations, creating meaningful reflection rituals, and noticing patterns early, you build the tools to grow alongside one another while staying connected to what matters most.

If you want to continue your journey toward alignment, there are many ways to deepen your connection and build on what you've learned through this book. Below are recommended next steps for couples who want to explore even further.

Attend a Relationship Workshop or Retreat

Workshops and retreats provide couples with a chance to step away from everyday routines and focus entirely on their relationship. These immersive experiences offer structured guidance, expert insights, and time for reflection, allowing partners to deepen their connection and gain new tools for maintaining alignment.

- Communication Workshops:
  - Learn tools for effective communication and conflict resolution, building the skills needed to navigate challenges with empathy.
  - **Example:** A workshop on active listening can help partners understand each other's needs more deeply, reducing misunderstandings and fostering emotional intimacy.
- Couples Retreats:
  - Spend a weekend or longer at a dedicated retreat center, focusing on shared goals, intimacy, and quality time without distractions. Many retreats include guided activities, exercises, and group discussions to promote deeper connection.
  - **Example:** A retreat that combines outdoor activities with relationship exercises to help couples bond while exploring nature.

- **Financial Planning for Couples:**
    - o Attend workshops that focus on financial alignment, offering tools for budgeting, saving, and aligning long-term financial goals.
    - o **Example:** A workshop might help couples build communication strategies around money, reducing tension around budgeting and spending.

Why It Works: Workshops and retreats create a focused environment for growth, allowing couples to explore new strategies for connection and build deeper emotional intimacy. These experiences also provide expert guidance, offering insights that are difficult to gain through everyday conversations.

Join a Community of Like-Minded Couples

Surrounding yourself with other couples on a similar path provides encouragement, insight, and a sense of community. Whether online or in-person, engaging with other couples helps normalize challenges and provides a supportive space for sharing experiences.

- **Online Forums:**
    - o Join communities where couples discuss personal growth, goal-setting, relationship alignment, and conflict resolution. These forums offer inspiration and tools for maintaining alignment, as well as a space to ask questions and share wins.
    - o **Example:** Participate in an online community focused on intentional living, where couples exchange ideas about balancing priorities and achieving shared goals.

- Support Groups:
    - o For couples navigating specific challenges—like parenting, retirement, or blended families—support groups offer strategies, insights, and encouragement. These groups help couples feel less isolated in their struggles and provide actionable advice from others who have been through similar situations.
    - o **Example:** A parenting support group can provide valuable tips for balancing career, family time, and personal goals.

Why It Works: Connecting with other couples creates a sense of accountability and encouragement. Being part of a community helps partners feel motivated and less alone in their journey toward alignment, while also offering practical insights for navigating challenges.

Consider Working with a Relationship Coach or Therapist

Sometimes, couples encounter challenges that feel too complex to navigate on their own. In these situations, working with a relationship coach or therapist can provide personalized strategies and support for overcoming obstacles and deepening alignment.

- Relationship Coaches:
    - o Coaches focus on practical goal-setting and help couples clarify priorities, improve communication, and create actionable plans for growth.
- Couples Therapists:
    - o Therapists specialize in emotional healing and conflict resolution. They can help partners address

      deep-seated issues, improve intimacy, and build trust.

- **When to Seek Help:**
  - o If recurring conflicts feel overwhelming or if you're struggling to align your priorities, professional guidance can help you move forward with greater clarity and connection.

Why It Works: A professional relationship coach or therapist provides unbiased insights and structured support tailored to your unique situation. Their guidance can help couples break through obstacles, strengthen emotional connection, and create a path toward sustainable alignment.

Bringing It All Together

Ongoing learning and community support are essential to maintaining alignment in your relationship. Whether through workshops, retreats, books, podcasts, or professional coaching, these resources provide inspiration, structure, and accountability. They remind couples that alignment is not just a one-time achievement—it's an ongoing quest that requires reflection, growth, and intentional effort.

By engaging with these tools and communities, you and your partner will have the resources you need to thrive together—learning, growing, and staying connected through every season of life.

A Journey Toward Intentional Love and Balance

The journey toward intentional alignment isn't always easy, but it's incredibly rewarding. By working through the Prioritize Us system, you've taken meaningful steps toward creating a relationship that reflects what truly matters to both of you. Every conversation, every goal, and every small action brings you closer to a life of purpose, connection, and balance.

Remember, alignment isn't about perfection—it's about learning, growing, and adjusting together as life unfolds. There will be moments of joy, and there will be challenges, but with intentional effort, your relationship will continue to evolve in beautiful ways.

This is just the beginning. The best relationships aren't static—they're dynamic, full of exploration, and deeply intentional. The work you've done here will serve as a roadmap for the rest of your journey together. Whenever life shifts or priorities change, you have the tools to realign, reconnect, and keep moving forward.

Align your love. Align your life. Prioritize Us.

The Research Behind Prioritize Us

Why do some couples thrive while others struggle despite love and mutual attraction? Research in psychology and relationship science suggests that one key factor lies in value alignment—the extent to which partners share similar priorities, beliefs, and goals. When partners' values align, they are better equipped to build trust, navigate conflicts, and foster long-term connection. Below, we explore the research behind shared values and how they shape relationship success.

Shared Values Foster Relationship Satisfaction

A study published in the Journal of Marriage and Family found that shared values are strongly correlated with higher relationship satisfaction. Couples who reported aligning on core values—such as family priorities, finances, and personal growth—were more likely to feel supported by their partners and less likely to experience chronic conflicts (Lee & Ono, 2012). This alignment creates a sense of partnership, as both individuals feel they are working toward common goals.

Additionally, research from Dr. Benjamin Karney, a renowned relationship psychologist, indicates that couples who share values tend to experience fewer disagreements about major life decisions, such as career choices or parenting styles. In these relationships, partners are more likely to interpret each other's behavior as cooperative rather than antagonistic, reducing the likelihood of conflict escalation (Karney & Bradbury, 1995).

Value Misalignment Can Lead to Emotional Distance

On the flip side, value misalignment—when partners prioritize different things—can cause friction. A meta-analysis by researchers at the University of Amsterdam found that couples with divergent values were more prone to long-term dissatisfaction, especially if they failed to communicate effectively about their differences (Van Lange et al., 2017). Partners may misinterpret each other's priorities, leading to feelings of being misunderstood, unappreciated, or unsupported.

For example, a partner who prioritizes career growth may feel they are working for the relationship's financial stability, while the other partner may interpret the long work hours as emotional neglect. Without understanding each other's motivations, these value misalignments can create emotional distance and recurring arguments, weakening the relationship over time (Gordon & Chen, 2016).

Shared Goals Strengthen Commitment and Trust

Another key benefit of shared values lies in their ability to strengthen commitment. Research published in Personal Relationships found that couples with aligned goals tend to experience greater emotional intimacy and trust (Weigel & Ballard-Reisch, 2002). Shared goals provide a sense of direction and purpose, making it easier for partners to coordinate their actions and support each other's efforts. This mutual support creates a positive feedback loop: the more aligned the partners feel, the more willing they are to invest in the relationship.

Interestingly, even couples with differing individual interests—such as hobbies or career ambitions— can thrive if they align on broader life values. This suggests that couples don't need to match in every area to succeed, but rather need to understand and respect each other's core values.

The Role of Value Alignment in Conflict Resolution

Research from Dr. John Gottman, a leading expert on relationship dynamics, highlights the importance of shared values in conflict resolution. In his decades-long studies of couples, Gottman found that those who aligned on their values were better able to engage in constructive conflict—expressing their frustrations without triggering defensiveness or contempt (Gottman & Silver, 1999). Shared values provide a foundation for empathy, helping partners view conflicts as opportunities to understand each other rather than as threats to the relationship.

Couples with aligned values are also more likely to engage in collaborative problem-solving, working together to find solutions that honor both partners' priorities. This collaborative mindset fosters emotional safety, making it easier for couples to address disagreements without damaging their connection.

Why Shared Values Matter

The research is clear: shared values play a crucial role in relationship satisfaction, emotional intimacy, and long-term success. While no two partners will align perfectly on every priority, the key lies in understanding each other's values and working intentionally to balance them. Couples who invest in aligning their values—whether through intentional conversations, collaborative goal-setting, or empathy-based conflict resolution—are better equipped to navigate life's challenges and strengthen their connection over time.

This is exactly where the Prioritize Us Test offers insight. By identifying where your priorities align and where they diverge, the test provides the clarity needed to foster meaningful conversations and intentional alignment. Backed by relationship science, the principles in this book empower couples to turn misalignment into an opportunity for growth—building trust, connection, and shared purpose along the way.

References

- Gordon, A. M., & Chen, S. (2016). Do you get where I'm coming from? Perceived understanding buffers against the negative impact of conflict on relationship satisfaction. Journal of Personality
- and Social Psychology, 110(2), 239-260.
- Gottman, J., & Silver, N. (1999). The Seven Principles for Making Marriage Work. Crown Publishing Group.
- Karney, B. R., & Bradbury, T. N. (1995). The longitudinal course of marital quality and stability: A review of theory, methods, and research. Psychological Bulletin, 118(1), 3-34.

- Lee, K. S., & Ono, H. (2012). Marriage, cohabitation, and happiness: A cross-national analysis of values and relationships. Journal of Marriage and Family, 74(5), 993-1012.
- Van Lange, P. A. M., Rusbult, C. E., Drigotas, S. M., & Arriaga, X. B. (2017). Commitment and interdependence in close relationships: An interdependence analysis. Journal of Social and Personal Relationships, 34(4), 563-589.
- Weigel, D. J., & Ballard-Reisch, D. S. (2002). Investigating the behavioral indicators of relational commitment. Personal Relationships, 9(2), 187-203.

Expanded Priority List

While the Prioritize Us Test focuses on the 10 core priorities— Career, Communication, Entertainment, Finances, Growth, Health, Relationships, Safety, Sex, and Spirituality—every individual and couple is unique. You may find that other priorities feel more relevant to your life. This expanded list offers additional priorities to help you customize your test results and reflect on areas that might hold deeper meaning for you and your partner. Feel free to swap out any of the original 10 priorities or add your own personal priorities to better align with your relationship.

Expanded Priority List

Adventure and Travel

- Do you value exploring new places and experiencing different cultures? Adventure might be a top priority if you thrive on novelty and spontaneity.

Creativity and Artistic Expression

- Whether it's through art, writing, music, or other forms of expression, this priority reflects a need for creative outlets and inspiration.

Environmental Responsibility

- If you feel strongly about sustainability and caring for the environment, this may be an essential shared value.

Family and Parenting

- This priority reflects a focus on raising children or nurturing family connections beyond the relationship.

Friendship and Social Life

- For those who place high value on social connections, friendships, and community, this priority reflects the need to nurture those relationships.

Learning and Education

- Lifelong learning, professional development, or personal enrichment might be priorities if you're always seeking knowledge and new skills.

Philanthropy and Giving Back

- If contributing to charity, volunteering, or giving back to your community is important, this priority reflects a focus on impact and contribution.

Independence and Personal Freedom

- Some people value autonomy—the freedom to make independent decisions and maintain personal space within the relationship.

Pets and Animal Care

- For pet owners, caring for animals may be a significant priority that requires time, effort, and shared responsibility.

Spontaneity and Fun

- Some people thrive on spontaneity, valuing unplanned adventures, humor, and light-hearted experiences.

Work-Life Integration

- If balancing work and personal life is a struggle, this priority emphasizes the importance of achieving harmony between professional and personal goals.

Justice and Activism

- This reflects a passion for social justice, activism, and advocating for change in the world.

How to Customize Your Prioritize Us Test

Customization allows you to tailor the Prioritize Us Test to reflect your unique relationship dynamics and life circumstances. The original ten priorities provide a solid foundation, but no two couples are exactly alike. By selecting priorities that resonate most with you, you can ensure that the test provides insights that feel relevant, actionable, and aligned with your specific goals. Customization also allows you to adapt the test over time, reflecting the natural shifts in your priorities as life evolves.

1. Select Custom Priorities

The first step in customizing your test is to identify which priorities resonate most with you and your partner. Review the expanded list of potential priorities (like parenting, work-life balance, or activism) and choose the ones that feel most meaningful at this stage of life.

- **How to Customize:**
    - o Replace one of the original ten priorities with a custom priority that reflects your circumstances more accurately.
    - o **Example:** If work-life balance feels more relevant to your relationship than "Career," swap the priority to better align with your needs.
- **Tips for Choosing Custom Priorities:**
    - o Focus on what matters right now. Are there priorities you feel need more attention?
    - o Use your Total Difference Score (TDS) as a guide. If one area consistently shows misalignment, it may be worth adding or adjusting a priority related to that area.

Why It Works: Selecting custom priorities ensures that the test reflects the specific areas of focus that matter most to you. This makes the results more meaningful, helping you create goals that directly address your current challenges and aspirations.

2. Use Context-Specific Priorities

If you and your partner are navigating a major life phase or transition, customizing your priorities can provide deeper insights into your relationship. Different life experiences—like parenthood, career shifts, or relocation—create new demands, and your priorities should reflect these changing realities.

- Examples of Context-Specific Priorities:
    - **Parenting:** Include priorities like "Family Time" or "Self-Care" to reflect the realities of raising children.
    - **Career Transitions:** Add priorities such as "Professional Growth" or "Work-Life Balance" to address changes in job demands.
    - **Relocation:** If you've recently moved, you may prioritize "Community Involvement" or "Building New Relationships" to reflect your focus on integrating into a new environment.
- How to Use Context-Specific Priorities:
    - Talk openly with your partner about how your circumstances are influencing your priorities and what changes might be needed to stay aligned.
    - **Example:** After becoming parents, you might add "Intimacy" as a custom priority to ensure that physical and emotional connection doesn't get lost amidst family responsibilities.

Why It Works: Using context-specific priorities helps you adapt the test to your current season of life. It ensures that your relationship conversations are rooted in the realities you're facing and reflect the areas where alignment is most needed.

3. Revisit Your Priorities Regularly

Priorities aren't static—they evolve over time as your goals, experiences, and circumstances shift. Regularly revisiting your customized priorities ensures that the test remains relevant and aligned with where you are as a couple. What was once a major focus—like career advancement—may later become less important, while new areas of focus, such as health or family, take center stage.

- **How to Revisit and Adjust Your Priorities:**
    - o Schedule time every month to reflect on your current priorities and see if any adjustments are needed.
    - o Use your TDS results as a guide—if certain priorities continue to show misalignment, it may be time to reassess or reframe them.
    - o Example: After a year of saving aggressively, financial security may no longer be a top priority, and you might decide to shift your focus toward travel or personal growth.
- **Questions to Guide Priority Reassessment:**
    - o "Are these priorities still aligned with our current values and goals?"
    - o "Have any new areas become more important in our lives?"
    - o "Is there a priority we're neglecting that deserves more attention?"

Why It Works: Regularly revisiting your priorities helps you stay proactive and intentional as your relationship evolves. It ensures that your actions remain aligned with what matters most and that both partners feel seen and supported as priorities shift.

Personalized Alignment for Long-Term Success

The beauty of the Prioritize Us Test lies in its flexibility and adaptability. By customizing your priorities, you create a version of the test that reflects the unique circumstances and needs of your relationship. Using context-specific priorities ensures that the insights you gain are relevant and actionable for your current season of life, while regularly revisiting your priorities allows you to grow together as your goals evolve.

Example: Creating a Custom Priority List

Here's an example of how a couple might customize their list to reflect their unique priorities:

Custom Priority List
1. Career
2. Health
3. Adventure and Travel
4. Family and Parenting
5. Communication
6. Romance and Emotional Intimacy
7. Learning and Education
8. Financial Stability
9. Environmental Responsibility
10. Creativity and Artistic Expression

In this example, the couple swapped "Entertainment" for "Adventure and Travel" and added "Family and Parenting" to reflect their current life stage. These adjustments ensure that the test feels meaningful and relevant to their specific needs and goals.

The beauty of the Prioritize Us System lies in its flexibility. Your relationship is unique, and your priorities should reflect your individual and shared values. Use this expanded list to make the test your own and revisit your priorities regularly as life evolves. By doing so, you'll ensure that the conversations you have and the goals you set are always aligned with what matters most to both of you.

This customization process deepens the meaning of the test and makes it even more powerful as a tool for growth and connection. Remember—alignment isn't a one-size-fits-all solution. It's about discovering what works best for your relationship and adjusting as you grow together.

Worksheets and Templates

This section provides easy-to-use worksheets and templates to help you and your partner stay organized and intentional throughout your journey. Whether you want to rank your priorities, calculate your Total Difference Score (TDS), or set actionable goals, these printable tools will guide you through every step of the process. Feel free to photocopy these pages, print them out, or access them digitally through the companion website or app.

1. Priority Ranking Worksheet

Use this worksheet to rank the 10 core priorities individually. Once both partners have completed their rankings, compare them to calculate your TDS and identify areas of alignment and misalignment.

Instructions:

- Rank each priority from 1 to 10 (1 being the most important, 10 being the least).
- Compare your rankings with your partner's to find the differences between corresponding priorities.

Nick Brancato

Priority	Your Rank	Partner's Rank	Difference
Career			
Communication			
Entertainment			
Finances			
Growth			
Health			
Relationships			
Safety			
Sex			
Spirituality			

2. Total Difference Score (TDS) Calculation Worksheet

This worksheet helps you calculate your Total Difference Score (TDS). Once both partners have listed their rankings, subtract each pair's rank to get the difference for that priority. Add up all the differences to find your TDS.

Instructions:

- For each priority, subtract one partner's ranking from the other to find the difference.
- Sum the differences across all 10 priorities to get your TDS.

Priority	Difference (Your Rank - Partner's Rank)
Career	
Communication	
Entertainment	
Finances	
Growth	
Health	
Relationships	
Safety	
Sex	
Spirituality	
Total Difference Score (TDS):	

3. Goal-Setting Worksheet

Use this worksheet to turn your priorities into actionable goals. Each partner can list individual goals, and together you can create shared goals to align your relationship.

Instructions:

- Identify 1-2 goals for each priority based on your rankings and TDS.

- Use the SMART goal framework (Specific, Measurable, Achievable, Relevant, Time-bound) to make each goal actionable.

Priority	Our Goal (SMART Framework)	Who's Responsible?	Deadline
Career			
Communication			
Entertainment			
Finances			
Growth			
Health			
Relationships			
Safety			
Sex			
Spirituality			

4. Progress Tracker Template

This tracker will help you and your partner monitor progress toward your goals over time. Regular check-ins will ensure you stay aligned and adjust your goals as needed.

Instructions:

- Use this template during weekly, monthly, or quarterly check-ins to track your progress.
- Include notes on what's working well, what challenges you've faced, and any adjustments you plan to make.

Date	Goal or Priority	Progress Update	Challenges or Adjustments Needed

5. Conflict Resolution Template

This template helps couples work through areas of conflict or misalignment identified through the TDS and goal-setting process.

Instructions:

- Identify a priority or conflict area where you and your partner are struggling.
- Use the resolution prompts to brainstorm solutions and create a plan for moving forward.

Conflict Resolution Worksheet

- Priority or Conflict Area:

_____

- How does this conflict impact us?

_____

- What do I need from my partner in this area?

  _____

- What can I offer my partner to help resolve the conflict?

  _____

- Our Solution or Compromise:

  _____

- Next Check-In Date: _____

How to Use These Worksheets Effectively

1. Schedule Regular Check-Ins:

- Set a recurring time (weekly, monthly, or quarterly) to review your progress and adjust goals as needed.

2. Keep It Collaborative:

- Use these worksheets together—goal-setting and alignment are most effective when both partners feel involved.

3. Celebrate Wins Along the Way:

- Acknowledge progress and celebrate both small and big victories. Positive reinforcement strengthens your commitment to alignment.

These worksheets and templates provide the practical structure you need to stay aligned, track progress, and maintain intentional connection. By filling out these pages together, you'll gain clarity, accountability, and deeper understanding—ensuring that your priorities are not only discussed but actively reflected in your actions.

Remember: Alignment is a journey, not a destination. Use these tools to adjust, grow, and celebrate your progress every step of the way.

APPENDIX C

The Evolution of Priorities and the Timeless Role of Values

The word "priority" traces back to the Latin word prior, meaning "former" or "first", denoting something that takes precedence over all else. For centuries, "priority" was a singular concept—there could only be one most important thing. It was only in the 20th century that the plural form, "priorities," emerged in the English language, reflecting the complexity of modern life and our growing tendency to juggle multiple competing concerns

This linguistic evolution marks a profound shift in how individuals and societies think about focus, decision-making, and the allocation of attention.

Today, people often speak of having many "priorities," but the original meaning of the word reminds us of a fundamental truth: not everything can be most important. This insight is central to the framework presented in Prioritize Us, where we explore how individuals and couples can align on what truly matters—not by trying to prioritize everything, but by identifying the few things that deserve first place in their lives.

The Distinction Between Values and Priorities

While the terms values and priorities are often used interchangeably, they represent distinct aspects of human behavior and thought. Values refer to enduring principles or beliefs that guide behavior over time. They are relatively stable, providing a moral compass that shapes how individuals interpret the world and make decisions. Thinkers from Plato to Kant have examined the concept of values, engaging with questions like "What virtues should we cultivate to lead meaningful lives?" Values have been studied for millennia in the realms of philosophy, religion, and ethics, underscoring their role as a foundation for human action

Priorities, by contrast, are fluid and context-dependent. They reflect what demands attention at any given moment—the actionable expression of values in a particular situation. Values provide the "why," while priorities provide the "what now." For example, someone who values health may prioritize exercise today, while tomorrow they may need to focus on rest. Priorities shift based on circumstances, relationships, and time horizons, requiring continual reflection and recalibration.

Values are the foundation for decision-making, while priorities are the expression of those values in action.

Values: A Longstanding Philosophical Inquiry

The exploration of values as a philosophical concept can be traced back to Ancient Greece, where thinkers like Aristotle identified virtues such as courage, wisdom, and justice as essential to living well. Later, Stoic philosophers in Ancient Rome emphasized the importance of aligning one's actions with reason and nature, valuing self-discipline and integrity. Medieval

Nick Brancato

theologians added spiritual dimensions to values, focusing on virtues like faith and charity.

In the modern era, philosophers during the Enlightenment began questioning traditional values and developed new frameworks centered around individual freedom, reason, and scientific inquiry. This history reveals how values serve as enduring touchstones, helping people navigate life's uncertainties across different cultural and historical contexts

A Framework for Modern Prioritization

In a world that increasingly demands us to manage competing interests—family, career, personal growth—the evolution from "priority" to "priorities" reflects the complexity of modern life. However, the proliferation of priorities also introduces confusion. Without clear alignment, people risk becoming overwhelmed, leading to stress, disconnection, and burnout. Prioritize Us bridges this gap by offering a systematic approach to prioritization, helping individuals and couples clarify what matters most and act on it with intention.

At its core, this book is about more than productivity—it's about living in alignment with your deepest values. As life shifts and priorities evolve, the goal is not to do more but to stay connected to what matters—to yourself, to your partner, and to your shared vision for the future. The ancient wisdom of values, coupled with the modern necessity of prioritization, offers a path to meaningful living in today's fast-paced world.

Keep Growing, Keep Aligning

Thank you for joining us on this journey toward greater alignment and intentional living. Throughout this book, you've explored the importance of shared priorities, meaningful conversations, and

228

actionable goals—all aimed at building a relationship that reflects what matters most to both of you. Alignment isn't a one-time achievement; it's an ongoing process of reflection, adjustment, and growth as life evolves.

We hope the tools, stories, and strategies in these pages have brought clarity, connection, and inspiration to your relationship. Whether you've redefined priorities, uncovered areas of misalignment, or set new goals together, each small step you take toward intentional alignment strengthens your bond and brings you closer to the life you want to build as a couple.

The Power of Sharing What Works

If this book has resonated with you—if it's helped you better understand your partner, feel more aligned, or navigate conflict more effectively—the best way to say "thank you" is by sharing it with someone else. Please tell other people about this book. Relationships thrive when we spread the tools and resources that help us grow.

Consider buying a copy for a friend, family member, or another couple who might benefit from the ideas in these pages. Sometimes, a single conversation about priorities or intentional living can spark lasting change. By sharing this book, you can inspire others to deepen their connection and build alignment in their own lives. You never know how far the ripple effect of one thoughtful gift can go.

THANK YOU FOR LETTING US BE PART OF YOUR JOURNEY

We're honored to have been part of your journey toward greater alignment and connection.

Remember, it's not about achieving perfection—it's about growing together with intention, empathy, and love. Life will continue to shift and change, but with the tools you've gained, you're ready to face every challenge and opportunity as a team.

Here's to building a relationship rooted in purpose, growth, and joy. Stay intentional, keep growing, and never stop aligning.

To stay connected and explore more personal development tools, feel free to **follow or contact me on Instagram:** @PersonalDevCoach.

ABOUT THE AUTHOR

Nick Brancato

(@PersonalDevCoach)

Nick Brancato has spent over 25 years transforming the way people connect, communicate, and thrive. As a Personal Development Coach and educator, Nick specializes in helping individuals and couples align their priorities and navigate life's challenges together—whether balancing career shifts, financial pressures, or personal growth.

Nick holds a Master's Degree in Education and has extensive experience designing transformative learning experiences. His unique blend of practical tools and insightful frameworks is rooted in both research and real-world application, drawing on his background as a Microsoft Systems Engineer.

This combination allows Nick to offer structured, data-driven approaches—like the *Total Difference Score (TDS)* in *Prioritize Us*—that guide couples through complex decisions with clarity and precision.

Inspired by both his professional work and personal experiences, Nick developed Prioritize Us to address a need he saw repeatedly: relationships fail not from a lack of love but from misaligned

Nick Brancato

priorities. This passion to empower others also shines through in his 40-video HowCast series on YouTube, which has amassed over 13 million views, helping people turn knowledge into action.

Beyond coaching, Nick integrates meditation, guided visualization, and hypnotherapy into his practice, believing that lasting change requires both emotional insight and practical steps. His approach nurtures deeper connection, mental clarity, and shared growth, helping couples move from tension to trust and from misalignment to mutual success.

Through *Prioritize Us*, Nick invites couples at every stage— whether newlyweds or long-term partners —to live with intention, align their values, and build a life that honors what matters most. His mission is simple: to help people grow together with purpose, connection, and clarity.